A Field Manual of Acoustic Phonetics

Senior Editor
George Huttar

Content Editors
Ronda Hartell-Jones
Eugene Loos
Mary Ruth Wise

Copy Editors
Bonnie Brown
Lana Martens

Production Staff
Compositor, Karoline Fisner
Graphic Artist, Barbara Alber

A Field Manual of Acoustic Phonetics

Joan L. G. Baart

SIL International
Dallas, Texas

© 2010 by SIL International
Library of Congress Catalog No.: 2009921503
ISBN: 978-1-55671-232-6

Printed in the United States of America

An earlier edition was released in LinguaLinks 5.0 as *Acoustic Phonetics* by Joan Baart, copyright 2002, SIL International.

Copies of this and other publications of SIL International
may be obtained from

International Academic Bookstore
7500 West Camp Wisdom Road
Dallas, TX 75236-5699

Voice: 972-708-7404
Fax: 972-708-7363
Email: academic_books@sil.org
Internet: http/www.ethnologue.com

Contents

1

Introduction

1.1 What is acoustic phonetics?

Phonetics is the scientific study of speech sounds. Traditionally, three domains of phonetics are distinguished:

- *Articulatory phonetics* studies how speech sounds are produced by a speaker.
- *Auditory phonetics* studies how speech sounds are perceived by a listener.
- *Acoustic phonetics* studies the properties of the sound waves that are associated with speech sounds.

Sound waves are small, rapid vibrations of air that start at one location and spread throughout a body of air. These vibrations can be captured by a microphone and stored on different media such as a magnetic tape or a computer disk. They can also be analyzed, displayed, and measured in various ways. For instance, a sound wave graph (also called a waveform graph or oscillogram) shows how the vibrations of the air develop over a period of time. Different sounds (vowels, consonants) are associated with different vibration patterns, and a great deal can be learned about them by studying these patterns.

The vibration patterns associated with speech sounds are actually very complex. These complex vibrations can be represented as consisting of many simple vibrations that are all occurring at the same time. Some of these simple vibrations are relatively slow (they are said to have a low frequency of vibration), while other vibrations are relatively fast (they have a high frequency of vibration); some vibrations are relatively weak (the size of the vibration, also called amplitude, is small), other vibrations are relatively strong (they have a large amplitude).

A SPECTRUM is a kind of graph that shows the composition of a complex sound at a certain moment in time in terms of simple vibrations; that is, it shows what vibration frequencies are present in a certain complex sound wave, and how strong these vibrations are. A SPECTROGRAM shows the same information (frequency and amplitude of the simple vibrations that make up a complex

1

sound), but it has a time dimension as well; in other words, a spectrogram shows how the spectral composition of a sound changes over time. (See chapter 3 for examples of spectrograms and spectra.)

Some sounds (such as voiced vowels) have a regular pattern of vibration. Though this pattern may be quite complex, it can be seen to repeat itself. The frequency of repetition of this complex pattern is called the FUNDAMENTAL FREQUENCY of the sound wave. Fundamental frequency is closely connected with the perception of pitch. Normally, a higher fundamental frequency corresponds to a higher perceived pitch, and a lower fundamental frequency corresponds to a lower perceived pitch. Fundamental frequency can be extracted from a speech wave (not always without error, though) and shown in a graph as a function of time.

All these and other techniques of analyzing, displaying, and measuring speech waves are part of the field of acoustic phonetics. Acoustic phonetics is not just concerned with the production of such data, but, more importantly, with the interpretation of the data thus produced. It tries to understand the relationship between the shape and the movements of the articulators on the one hand, and the properties of the speech wave (the acoustic signal) on the other. It also tries to understand the relationship between the properties of the acoustic signal and the sounds as perceived by the listener.

1.2 Benefits of acoustic phonetics for linguistic fieldwork

Acoustic phonetics has several potential benefits for linguistic fieldwork.

To start with, acoustic analysis may help improve the accuracy of phonetic transcriptions. Some people find certain phonetic distinctions difficult to hear with their ears alone. Examples of such distinctions are

- relative pitch height (high, mid, low),
- the direction of pitch movements (rising or falling),
- relative length (duration) of vowels and consonants,
- differences in vowel quality,
- presence versus absence of aspiration, and
- voice quality distinctions (regular voice, breathy voice, creaky voice).

Information gleaned from speech waveforms, spectrograms, fundamental frequency graphs (pitch graphs), and other representations of the acoustic signal, can supplement the ears-alone analysis and in this way increase the accuracy and precision of the phonetic description of the sounds of a language. Sometimes inspection of acoustic data may point to an altogether new analysis that one would have missed without the acoustic instruments.

A second benefit of the use of acoustic instruments is that one can take quantitative measurements, that is, measurements that can be expressed in the form of numbers, which can then be used for further statistical analysis. In this way, questions can be addressed that would be very difficult, if not impossible, to tackle with an ears-alone analysis; for example, whether larger units of connected text, such as paragraphs and sections, are systematically associated with certain patterns of pitch, loudness, duration, or speech rate, or whether the quality of a vowel has an influence on pitch height.

A third benefit is that "instruments allow permanent records to be made so that one can demonstrate the facts to those who do not have access to speakers of the language being described" (Ladefoged 1997:141). An analysis of a tone language, for example, can be corroborated by fundamental frequency graphs of a number of crucial examples, and these can be helpful when questions about the accuracy of the phonetic data arise.

In summary, use of acoustic instruments may add accuracy, precision, and objectivity to our phonetic descriptions; it may also lead us to hypotheses and solutions that we might not have thought of otherwise.

1.3 Acoustic phonetics and linguistic analysis

Acoustic phonetics does not take the place of phonological analysis. Neither do instrumental records take the place of impressionistic, auditory phonetic transcriptions. According to Ladefoged:

> It is surely true that by far the most valuable assets a phonetician can have are a trained set of ears. It is also true...that the ears should be coupled to highly trained vocal organs that are capable of producing a wide range of sounds. There is no substitute for the ability to hear small distinctions in sounds. There is also no substitute for the ability to pronounce alternative possibilities, so that one can ask a speaker which of two pronunciations sounds better. One of the most efficient procedures for getting results in the field is to test different hypotheses by trying out various vocal gestures of one's own. (p. 141)

In the same article, Ladefoged also says:

> The first requirement for a phonetic description of a language is a good account of the phonology. Of course, it is also true that in order to describe the phonology one needs to know the phonetics. The two things go hand in hand...Obviously they actually evolve together. But it is usually phonological knowledge that precedes detailed phonetic

observation. Some people still have a lingering feeling, based on older works such as Pike's (1947) Phonemics, that a linguist should go into the field, make detailed phonetic transcriptions of some speakers, and then sort out the sounds into phonemes. But it seldom works out like that. Only rarely does one notice a phonetic difference between two sounds in a corpus, and then examine the corpus to see if they are in contrast...After the phonological contrasts have been observed, then the phonetic differences involved can be described. (p. 138)

It is interesting to note that actually Pike made exactly the same point in a tone study on which he collaborated:

Normally...the analyst should plan to first make his linguistic, auditory, contrastive analysis of the system in sufficient detail to determine that contrasts exist in such and such places, between such and such utterances, and must contain so many—and no more—basic units or unit composites in the system. The analysis would be accomplished by frame techniques which allow such contrasts to be seen most readily, in contexts where conditioned and free variation are kept to a minimum. As these units are being determined, they would be described roughly, by crude auditory judgment, as to their phonetic characteristics of pitch, stress, length. *Once the units are thus clearly available for instrumental study, crucial examples would then ideally be chosen to be described accurately, with instrumental help.* (Pike, Barrett, and Bascom 1959:20–21; emphasis added)

All this is not to deny that acoustic phonetics can play, and in some cases has played, a crucial role in the solution of problems of phonetic and phonological description. However, a lack of understanding on the part of the fieldworker of how acoustic phonetics can contribute to the linguistic analysis, may lead to disappointment and even frustration.

1.4 The problem of interpreting acoustic data

A key problem in the application of acoustic analysis to linguistic description is this: the distinctions that are linguistically relevant, including the distinctions that are relevant to impressionistic, ears-only phonetic transcription, are usually not manifested in the acoustic signal (the sound waves) in a simple and straightforward fashion. Often there is not a simple correspondence between a certain phonetic or phonological feature (such as [+voice] or [+stressed]) and a single clearly identifiable property of the acoustic signal.

In the words of Fry (1968:371) "It is one of the basic facts about speech and language that there is never a one-to-one correlation between linguistic units and the characteristics of the articulatory, acoustic, or perceptual patterns with which they are associated."

Phoneticians, then, do not see speech sound as being a direct and complete acoustic expression of a string of phonological units. Rather they understand a speech wave as a series of cues: acoustic events that may trigger the perception of certain phonological features.

The presence of just one acoustic cue may sometimes not be sufficient to trigger the perception of a certain phonological feature. Often the acoustic signal associated with a certain utterance contains not one cue, but a cluster of acoustic cues that together strengthen each other's effect and help the listener discern the relevant phonological feature (see also Fujimura and Erickson 1997:71). In such a cluster of cues, some cues tend to be more important to perception than others so that one can speak of a hierarchy of cues. Since there may be quite a bit of variation from utterance to utterance, cues that are otherwise relatively unimportant may become important if another cue that is higher up in the hierarchy is not present. Section 4.2.1 of this manual (on the voiced-voiceless distinction) presents an instructive example of a phonological feature that is associated with a large cluster of potential acoustic cues.

Perception of speech is a process that is guided by higher-order knowledge, such as knowledge of the linguistic and situational context in which an utterance is spoken, and general knowledge of the world. Sometimes a listener recognizes a feature such as [+voice] in the absence of any relevant acoustic cue whatsoever, perhaps even ignoring cues that would otherwise lead to the perception of a [–voice] element. In such cases, the listener expects the [+voice] element to be there on the basis of this higher-order knowledge, and this expectation may override the information in the acoustic signal.

Because of this complex relationship between properties of the acoustic signal and linguistic features, the interpretation of acoustic data is not always simple. The field of acoustic phonetics has made a lot of progress during the last 60 to 70 years and has produced a vast literature. The purpose of this manual is to tap into that literature and make some of the findings of acoustic phonetics more easily accessible to fieldworkers.

1.5 Overview of the following chapters

As mentioned in section 1.1, from a physical point of view, sound exists in the form of vibrations that occur in a body of air, that is, as rapid alternating increases and decreases of air pressure. A microphone can register these air pressure fluctuations and convert them into electric voltage fluctuations. The voltage fluctuations can then be displayed—through various techniques—on a screen or on a piece of paper. A sound wave graph is a visual display of the acoustic signal that shows air pressure as a function of time (that is, it shows how air pressure fluctuates over a period of time); it is also called an oscillogram or waveform.

Sound wave graphs are the subject of chapter 2. We will look in some detail at what spoken utterances look like when they are represented in the form of sound wave graphs. We will observe that human speech basically consists of a sequence of "buzzes, hisses, and pops," interrupted by short periods of silence. We will see how these elementary sound events correspond, respectively, to periodic (regular) waves, random waves, and burst waves seen in a sound wave graph. We will then learn how to identify various major classes of speech sounds in a sound wave graph, such as vowels, voiced and voiceless plosives, aspirated plosives, fricatives, nasals, and other sonorants.

The sound wave graph is a useful display when one wants to determine segment boundaries in an utterance (the term SEGMENT is often used as an overall term for vowel and consonant sounds). Precise and consistent segmentation of an utterance can serve several purposes, and is particularly important when one wants to measure the duration of sounds or larger parts of the utterance. Therefore, the last section of chapter 2 presents a number of guidelines for determining segment boundaries in an utterance.

Chapter 3 is concerned with spectral analysis of speech. In spectral analysis, a complex sound wave is decomposed into a set of simple waves (sine waves) that have different amplitudes and vibration frequencies. The chapter discusses two kinds of displays: spectrograms (which have a time dimension) and spectra (which do not have a time dimension). A wealth of information about speech sounds can be obtained from spectrograms and spectra. The chapter presents a number of basic notions that are important for the study of spectrograms of speech, such as energy distribution, periodicity, harmonic structure, and formants. The chapter concludes with a discussion of the spectral characteristics of a number of major classes of speech sounds.

The remaining two chapters are devoted to more specific phonetic phenomena. Chapter 4 is concerned with voice quality and the voiced-voiceless distinction. It considers the question of how different voice qualities—notably regular voice, creaky voice, breathy voice, as well as voicelessness—are reflected in the acoustic signal. The second half of the chapter focuses on the contrast between voiced, voiceless, and aspirated plosives. It is shown, for example, that there is actually a cluster of acoustic events that correspond to the voiced-voiceless distinction, rather than one single acoustic property.

Chapter 5 deals with the preliminaries of analyzing prosodic features such as tone, stress, and intonation. The chapter discusses the relation between these linguistic features and the acoustic features of the signal, such as fundamental frequency, intensity, and duration. The chapter also shows how patterns of fundamental frequency, intensity, and duration in an utterance are the result of the interaction of a variety of factors. The researcher interested in tone, for example, will need to be able to disentangle these different influences on a fundamental frequency curve so as to get at the information that is relevant to studying tone.

2

Speech Waves

2.1 Sound waves: Time and amplitude

2.1.1 What is sound?

The air around us consists of numerous little particles. These air particles are not inactive; rather they are constantly moving back and forth, up and down, in an irregular, random fashion. Due to these random movements of the air particles, a surface (such as a sheet of paper, or the wall of a house, or a section of human skin) that is in contact with the air is constantly bombarded with particles that are colliding with it. The total impact of all these little collisions of air particles with a surface is called the PRESSURE of the air on that surface.

We can speak of air pressure in general, without referring to a specific surface that is in contact with the air. When we do this, we refer to the pressure that a certain body of air would exert on an arbitrary surface if it were brought in contact with it. As some surfaces are bigger than others, we need to be able to talk about air pressure, disregarding the size of the surface that may be undergoing this pressure. Therefore, air pressure is usually expressed in terms of the total impact that would be experienced by a surface of a certain standard size, for instance impact per square meter.

It is easy to see how air pressure is affected by the density of the air particles. When more particles are contained within the same space (for instance, one can blow or pump more air into a certain space), then also more particles will be colliding with a surface that is in contact with the air in that space, and so there will be more pressure on that surface. If air is sucked out of a container, then the number of air particles remaining inside the container is reduced and, therefore, the air pressure within that container is reduced.

From a physical point of view, sound consists of a series of small, rapid fluctuations of air pressure. Certain actions, such as slamming a book on a table or clapping one's hands, cause a displacement of air that disturbs the air pressure in the vicinity of the action. First, the air pressure will increase due to the inflow of air particles at that place (the air at that place is compressed). The next moment, air pressure will decrease again as the air tries to return to its original state. This "corrective" action may overshoot and result in a

9

state where the air pressure at that same place is actually below average (due to outflow of particles, the air in that place is rarefied). This then results in another increase of air pressure, followed by another decrease, until the fluctuations even out and a state of equilibrium is attained. The air, then, behaves like a metal spring: if you push it in (or pull it out) and release it, it will vibrate for some time until it has returned to its original state.

Fluctuations of air pressure in one location affect the air pressure in adjacent locations. The air pressure in these adjacent locations also starts to fluctuate, and these fluctuations in turn affect the air pressure in locations adjacent to them. In this way, air pressure fluctuations can spread throughout a body of air (although the fluctuations become smaller as the distance from the source becomes larger), and so sound may travel from its source (for instance, the place where a book was slammed on a table) to a human ear. The air pressure fluctuations, when they reach the ear, cause the eardrum to vibrate. When the air pressure on the outside of the eardrum is greater than the air pressure on the inside, the drum will be pushed in a little. When the air pressure on the outside of the eardrum is smaller than the air pressure on the inside, the drum will be pushed out a little. In this way, when a sound reaches the ear, it will cause vibrating movements of the eardrum. The ear converts these vibrations into electrochemical signals, which are then transmitted through the nerves to the brain and perceived as "sound."

2.1.2 Waveforms

The air pressure fluctuations that are associated with a sound can be registered by a microphone and converted into electrical voltages of fluctuating magnitudes, in such a way that the voltage fluctuations correspond to the air pressure fluctuations. With the help of electronic equipment, these fluctuations can be

- recorded,
- stored,
- analyzed,
- played back, and
- made visible in the form of graphs.

A standard personal computer, equipped with a sound card, microphone, loudspeakers, and software for acoustic analysis, is capable of performing all these functions.

In this chapter, we will look in particular at one type of graph, which is the sound wave graph (also called oscillogram or waveform). When

the sound involved is speech, I will often use the term SPEECH WAVE and
SPEECH WAVE GRAPH (or SPEECH WAVEFORM) rather than sound wave
and sound wave graph. A sound wave graph presents a picture of air pressure variations as recorded over a certain period of time. In the graph,
the horizontal dimension (the left-to-right dimension) represents TIME.
The vertical dimension (bottom-to-top) represents AIR PRESSURE. When
there is no sound, only a straight horizontal line is seen that represents
the average pressure of the air. When there is sound, a curve is seen that
goes up and down, fluctuating around the average value.

An example of a sound wave graph is shown in figure 2.1. The sound
involved is that produced by the slamming of a book on a table. Another
example is given in figure 2.2, which involves the speech wave of a part of
the vowel sound [o^u] taken from the word *boat* as spoken by the author. The
straight horizontal line that runs through the middle of the pictures represents the average value around which the air pressure fluctuates. As one can
see in figure 2.1, the slamming sound consists of a few major vibrations after
which the fluctuations quickly even out and return to silence. The major vibrations occur during the first 50 milliseconds of the sound (which is equal
to one-twentieth of a second), and silence is virtually regained after only 200
milliseconds (one-fifth of a second) from the beginning of the sound.

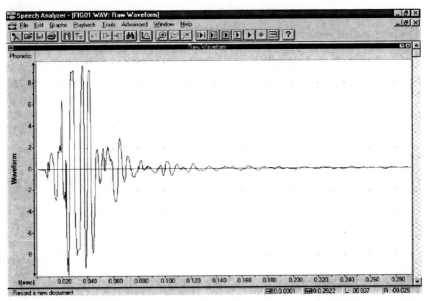

Figure 2.1. Sound wave graph representing the sound of a book slammed
on a table.

Figure 2.2 shows a complex pattern of vibrations consisting of major peaks with series of minor peaks in between, and with small vibrations riding on top of the larger vibrations. This complex pattern occurs six times within the section that is shown in the figure. The duration of the section shown is very short: less than 50 milliseconds. The duration of the vowel out of which this section was taken was approximately 200 milliseconds.

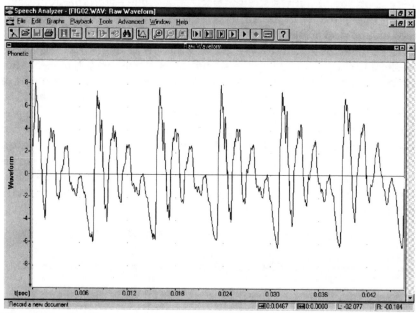

Figure 2.2. Speech wave graph of a section of the sound [oᵘ] taken from the word "boat" spoken by the author.

When sound is pictured in this way, the result is an undulating line: when we follow the curve from left to right in the graph, it keeps going up and down like the waves of the sea. This explains the use of the terms wave and waveform in connection with sound and speech.

A waveform represents deviations from average air pressure at successive points in time. At some points in time these deviations are POSITIVE (above average), and at other points they are NEGATIVE (below average). At some points they are relatively small and at other points they are relatively large. Peaks and valleys are points of the wave where a maximum positive or negative deviation is reached. The AMPLITUDE of a wave is equal to the largest deviation from average pressure. The deviation at the peak gives us the positive amplitude of a wave. Likewise, the deviation at the valley gives us the negative amplitude.

Normally, when we speak of amplitude we mean the largest deviation, disregarding whether this is a positive or a negative deviation.

Figure 2.3 presents an example of a simple wave. The average value around which the wave fluctuates is shown as a horizontal line (also called the ZERO LINE). In the figure, the positive and negative amplitudes are indicated. In this example, these are equal.

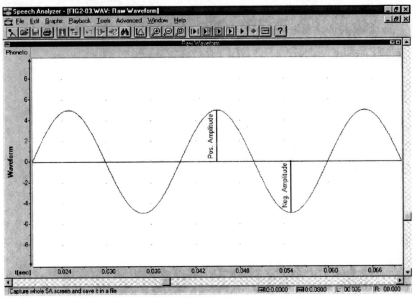

Figure 2.3. Positive and negative amplitude of a sound wave.

As stated above, waveforms (sound wave graphs) have two dimensions. The left-to-right dimension represents time (that is, a point more to the right in the graph represents a later moment in time). The bottom-to-top dimension represents air pressure (a point higher in the graph corresponds to a higher pressure). We will now begin to look at properties of the sounds of speech as they show up in waveforms. First of all, we will make some initial observations regarding the durations of speech sounds (measured along the horizontal dimension) and the amplitudes of speech sounds (measured along the vertical dimension).

Time

Figure 2.4 presents a waveform of the utterance *Say boat again.* The graph has been divided into segments that correspond to the consonant and vowel sounds that make up the utterance. The boundaries between the segments are indicated by means of vertical lines. On top of the graph, a phonetic transcription of each segment is provided. Below each segment, a number is given that represents the duration of that segment in milliseconds (a MILLISECOND is a thousandth of a second; I will use the abbreviation *ms* in this work).

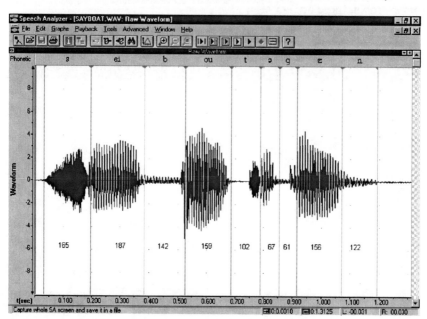

Figure 2.4. Speech wave graph with segment boundaries and phonetic transcription; segment durations are given in milliseconds.

The durations of the speech sounds in figure 2.4 are quite typical: the longer speech sounds have durations in the range of 150–200 ms. The longest sounds are usually stressed and/or long vowels. Sometimes nasals and fricatives (such as the [s] in figure 2.4) can also be quite long in duration. An unstressed and/or short vowel can be much shorter, such as the [ə] in figure 2.4. Examples of very short speech sounds (not seen in this example) are homorganic plosives (plosives preceded by another consonant that is produced at the same place of articulation) and the flapped [r]. These can be as short as 30 ms or less (Lehiste 1976, Shoup and Pfeifer 1976).

Very generally speaking, the average duration of a syllable is in the range of 200–300 ms, so three to five syllables will usually fit into one second.

Amplitude

Figure 2.5 displays the same utterance again, now focusing on the amplitudes of the waves that correspond to the different vowel and consonant sounds. There is a close correlation between the *loudness* of a sound as we perceive it, and its overall amplitude as shown in a waveform. Sounds that are perceived as relatively loud usually show relatively large amplitudes. In speech, the loudest sounds and, thus, the sounds with the largest overall amplitudes are usually the vowels. Next to vowels, nasals and liquids can also have relatively large amplitudes. The "sharp" voiceless fricatives [s] and [ʃ] can have amplitudes that are relatively large. Fricatives (other than [s] and [ʃ]) and plosives usually have relatively small amplitudes.

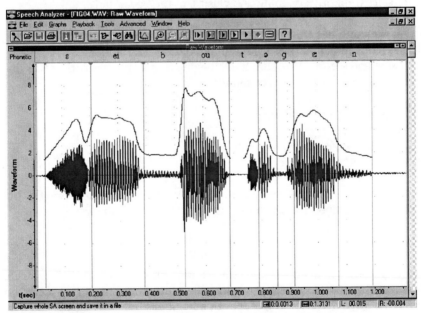

Figure 2.5. Signal amplitude plotted over a speech wave graph.

In figure 2.5, the curve plotted over the speech wave represents the amplitude as it changes over time (combining positive and negative amplitudes). As can be seen, the three stressed vowels have the largest amplitudes, the [s] and the [ə] have somewhat smaller amplitudes, and the three plosive consonants have yet smaller amplitudes. In this example, the nasal [n] also comes out with a relatively small amplitude, probably due to the fact that it occurs at the end of the utterance and the voice is falling away.

2.2 Four basic types of speech wave

For a further study of speech waveforms, it is useful to classify the elementary sounds of speech into four groups, based on the source from which they are derived:

- *Silence* (no sound; occurs as a part of a plosive consonant, and also in speech pauses)
- *Plosion* (sudden flow of air due to the build-up and subsequent release of a pressure difference)
- *Friction noise* (turbulence due to air that is forced through a narrow constriction)
- *Voice* (repetitive opening and closing of the vocal folds)

As someone has said, human speech is a sequence of buzzes (voicing), hisses (frication), and pops (plosion) (quoted in CSLU 2008).

Shoup and Pfeifer (1976) use the following terms for the speech waves that belong to these four classes of sounds:

1. Quiescent wave (silence)
2. Burst
3. Quasi-random wave
4. Quasi-periodic wave

For the sake of simplicity, we will use terms which are less precise, but easier to remember: silence, burst, random wave, periodic wave.

2.2.1 Silence

Short periods of silence or near-silence play an important role in speech. Silence is seen in a waveform as absence of fluctuations during a certain stretch of time. (A recording of speech may not be entirely "clean" and may contain background noise, echo, and so on. In such cases, periods of silence in the utterance under study may be more difficult to detect in a waveform.) Periods of silence during speech may be due to pausing, where the flow of speech is interrupted for a brief moment in order to give the listener some time to process what has been said so far, or, alternatively, to give the speaker some time to plan the next part of the sentence. Short periods of silence, however, also occur as a portion of voiceless plosives. An example of the latter is seen in figure 2.6, which represents the Dutch word *auto* 'car' as spoken by the author. In the figure, the arrow points to the period of silence (the silent interval) belonging to the closure phase of the voiceless plosive [t].

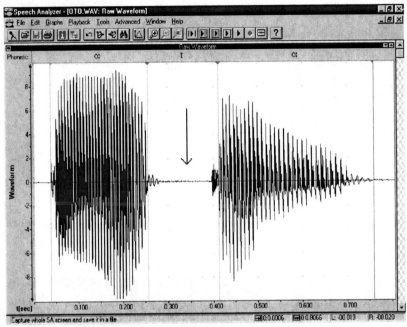

Figure 2.6. Silent interval of the voiceless plosive [t] spoken in the middle of the Dutch word *auto* 'car'.

2.2.2 Burst

A burst is a wave that is produced by a transient sound source: a momentary event that cannot be extended in time. An example is a slam on a table with a book, as in figure 2.1 above. In speech, burst-like waves are usually seen as parts of plosives, clicks, ejectives, and implosives. Figure 2.7 shows the word *auto* 'car' once more, this time drawing attention to the burst that corresponds to the release phase of the voiceless plosive [t]. Figure 2.8 shows the burst of the plosive [p], taken from the Dutch word *opa* 'granddad'. It can be seen in the figures that the durations of the bursts are very short: in between 15 and 20 ms for the cases shown in the figures.

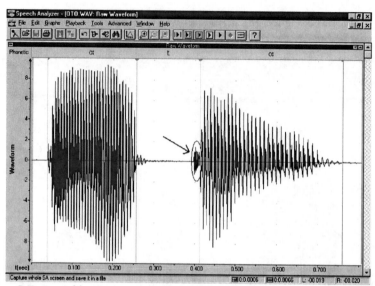

Figure 2.7. Sound burst (encircled) belonging to the plosive [t] in Dutch *auto* 'car'.

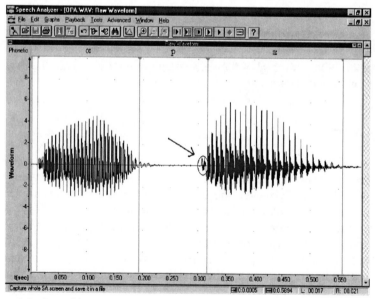

Figure 2.8. Sound burst (encircled) belonging to the plosive [p] in Dutch *opa* 'granddad'.

2.2.3 Random wave

Random speech waves are caused by turbulent airflow, as in fricatives. These sounds differ from bursts in that they can be sustained for some time. Random waves do not show a regular, recurring pattern. An example is given in figure 2.9, involving the voiceless fricative [ʃ] taken from the word *ship* spoken by the author.

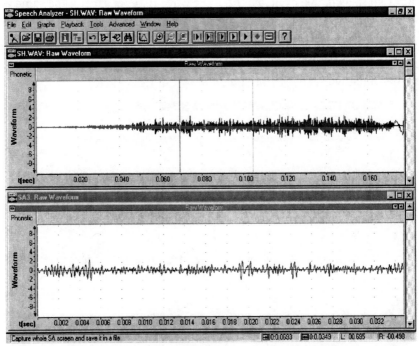

Figure 2.9. Random wave belonging to the voiceless fricative [ʃ] as spoken in the word *ship;* the lower panel zooms in on the part of the sound that is shown between the vertical lines in the upper panel.

It can be seen in the lower panel of figure 2.9 (which is an enlargement of the section shown between vertical lines in the upper panel) that the curve follows a random course. There are larger and smaller peaks, but their sizes and their occurrences in time appear to be totally unpredictable. One constant factor that we do see in this particular case is that the fluctuations are extremely rapid. In the lower panel, which represents only some 35 ms of time, the curve crosses the zero line (the horizontal line running through the middle) a great many times.

2.2.4 Periodic wave

(Quasi-) periodic waves show patterns that repeat themselves. It takes
a certain amount of time to complete the fluctuations that belong to a
pattern, and then another instance of the same pattern starts. The time
needed to complete one instance of the pattern (to complete one cycle) is
called the CYCLE PERIOD of the wave, or simply the PERIOD of the wave.
In actual speech, one cycle of a periodic wave is never exactly the same as
the next cycle. Still, when sections of a wave graph are approximately the
same for successive periods, that wave is said to be periodic. The sound
source of periodic speech waves is normally the vibration of the vocal
folds. An enlarged section of the speech wave of the vowel [a] as spoken
in the Dutch word *opa* 'granddad' is shown in figure 2.10.

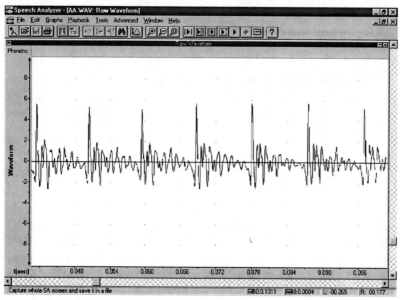

Figure 2.10. Periodic wave belonging to a portion of the vowel [a] as
spoken in Dutch *opa* 'granddad'.

Figure 2.10 shows a recurring pattern, consisting of one major peak and
nine minor peaks. The pattern repeats itself approximately every 9 ms; in
other words, the cycle period is 9 ms. The period of the speech wave corresponds to the rate of vibration of the vocal folds. The time taken to complete
one cycle of the speech wave is equal to the time taken by the vocal folds to
open and close one time.

It can also be seen that each successive cycle of the wave is slightly different from the preceding cycle. This is a reflection of the fact that the sound is not completely stationary. Rather in speech, the position and shape of the articulators (lips, tongue, jaw, and so forth) are constantly changing as they approach the targets associated with one sound and then continue to move on to assume the necessary positions for the next sound.

The perception of higher and lower pitch is related to the rate of vibration of the vocal folds, and to the periodicity of the speech wave. A smaller cycle period normally results in the perception of a higher pitch, and a longer period to the perception of lower pitch. When we count how many cycles would fit into one second, we arrive at the FUNDAMENTAL FREQUENCY of the speech wave at a certain point in time. For instance, if at a certain moment during the production of a vowel [a] it takes the speaker 9 ms to complete one cycle, then approximately 111 of such cycles would fit into one second (one second equals 1,000 ms). We say that at that point in the utterance, the fundamental frequency has a value of 111 cycles per second. Instead of "cycles per second," the term hertz (Hz) is more often employed in the literature to denote exactly the same thing. A cycle period of 9 ms, then, corresponds to a fundamental frequency of 111 Hz.

In principle, periodicity is seen in all sounds whose source is the vibration of the vocal folds. Therefore, not only vowels, but also (voiced) nasals, liquids, and semivowels show periodic speech waves. A little more complex are the cases of voiced plosives and voiced fricatives. During the release phase of voiced plosives and during the production of voiced fricatives, there are actually two sources of sound at work. On the one hand, the vocal folds are vibrating, and they produce a periodic speech wave. At the same time, air turbulence is produced at the place of articulation of the plosive or fricative, and this turbulence results in a burst or a random speech wave. In such cases then, periodic and aperiodic speech waves are combined into one speech wave. An example is given in figure 2.11. The sound shown is the voiced fricative [z] spoken in the Dutch word *ozon* 'ozone'.

Figure 2.11 clearly shows the dual nature of the [z]. On the one hand, we see the extremely rapid, random fluctuations that correspond to the friction noise that is generated at the point where the tongue approaches the alveolar ridge. On the other hand, if we try to disregard these rapid variations, we can discern a repetitive pattern for which we can even determine a cycle period. This repetitive (periodic) pattern corresponds to the buzzing sound that is generated by the vibrating vocal folds.

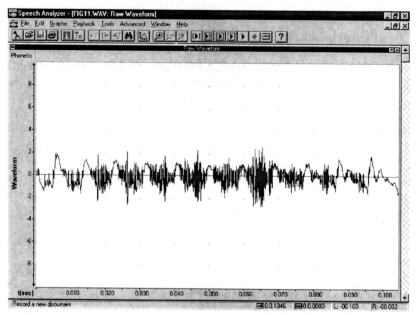

Figure 2.11. Speech wave corresponding to the voiced fricative [z] spoken in Dutch *ozon* 'ozone'.

2.3 Recognizing major types of speech sounds

When acoustic analysis of speech is used in linguistic fieldwork, it is normally not necessary to guess from a waveform what utterance it represents. Normally we know what the utterance is, and we are analyzing it to study one or another problematic feature that occurs at a certain point in the utterance. It is, nevertheless, useful for this type of study to develop the skill of distinguishing major types of speech sounds (vowels, plosives, fricatives, and so forth) from one another in speech waveforms. For instance, it is helpful to be able to see that some section of a graph corresponds to a vowel sound, and that another section corresponds to a voiceless plosive, even if one cannot tell from the graph whether the vowel is [i] or [a], or whether the plosive is [t] or [k]. With this skill, one will be able to quickly eyeball a graph and determine where the respective consonant and vowel sounds are located, and in particular where the word or sound is located that one wants to study in detail.

The following subsections are based on the discussion in a phonetics textbook by Rietveld and van Heuven (1997:113ff.).

2.3.1 Vowels

Figure 2.12 presents a waveform of an utterance in Kalam Kohistani, a language of northern Pakistan. The utterance is [aːska bɔːr mana] 'to-this Pathan they-call' ('this is called a Pathan'). Most of the vowels clearly stand out in the graph. They have a larger overall amplitude than the other sounds, and they have a longer duration than the other sounds. A section of the utterance, corresponding to the vowel [ɔː], is shown in the lower panel in the figure. In this lower panel, we can see the periodic structure of the vowel sound. There is a regular wave pattern that repeats itself 22 times in the graph (although it does change slightly with each successive period).

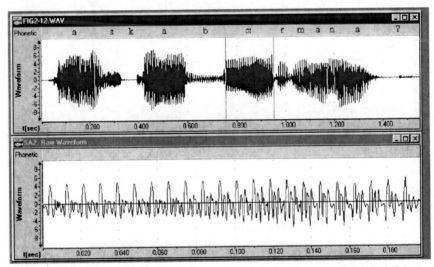

Figure 2.12. Kalam Kohistani utterance, with enlargement of the vowel [ɔː].

The same figure also shows a typical problem for the recognition of vowel sounds in a waveform. In the last word, two nasal consonants [m] and [n] occur that have a similar overall amplitude as the vowels of the word. It is difficult to say on the basis of a casual inspection of the graph which are the nasals and which are the vowels. An enlarged view of a vowel and a neighboring nasal may show a difference in the finer wave structure. Often the shape of the wave is smooth in the case of nasals, and more jagged in the case of vowels; see section 2.3.7 for an example.

2.3.2 Voiceless plosives

Figure 2.13 shows the same Kalam Kohistani utterance, this time with an enlargement of the voiceless plosive [k] in the lower panel.

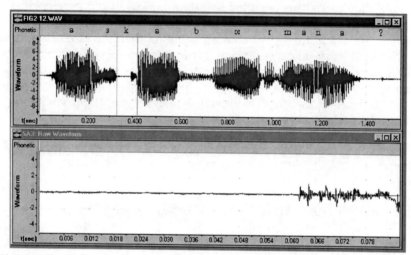

Figure 2.13. Kalam Kohistani utterance, with enlargement of the voiceless plosive [k].

There is a period of silence, corresponding to the closure phase of the voiceless plosive. In the example, the silent interval lasts for 62 ms. Following the silent interval, there is a relatively weak, aperiodic signal of a very short duration (24 ms in this example); this constitutes the burst that corresponds to the release of the plosive. Typically, silent intervals for voiceless plosives have durations up to 100 ms, while bursts can have durations in the range of 10 to 30 ms.

2.3.3 Voiced plosives

An example of a voiced plosive is taken out of the same utterance and presented in figure 2.14. During the closure phase of the voiced plosive (which is a [b] in this example), there is a weak buzzing sound as the vocal folds are still vibrating. This is seen in figure 2.14 as a periodic signal with a small overall amplitude (the lower panel presents an enlargement of the plosive). In this example, the closure phase has a duration of approximately 135 ms, which is quite long. In the case of voiced plosives, the burst corresponding to the release of the plosive may be difficult to find in the graph, as it may merge with the onset of a following vowel. At the place indicated by a vertical line in the lower panel of figure 2.14, the regularly undulating wave pattern belonging to the closure phase comes to an end. For a short moment, a few irregular vibrations are seen, and these correspond to the plosion noise of the [b]. The duration of this burst is quite short in the example: about 18 ms.

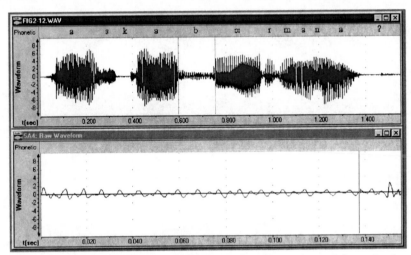

Figure 2.14. Kalam Kohistani utterance, with enlargement of the voiced plosive [b].

2.3.4 Voiceless aspirated plosives

The distinguishing feature of aspirated plosives is a delay between the burst and the onset of the following vowel. An example is seen in figure 2.15. The voiceless aspirated plosive [tʰ] is taken from the word [tʰun] 'pillar' in the Kalam Kohistani sentence [ĩː miːʃ tʰun maka paʃɑn] 'this man pillar to-me is-showing' ('this man is showing me a pillar').

In figure 2.15, the aspirated plosive is demarcated in the upper panel by the two vertical lines. The whole of the lower panel corresponds with exactly that section of the speech wave. As can be seen in the lower panel, the silent interval of the [tʰ] lasts for about 60 ms, which is a normal value. However, the aperiodic wave that follows the silent interval and continues until the start of the vowel, has a duration of approximately 85 ms. This is much longer than the usual 10–30 ms burst that we see in unaspirated plosives, and this leads us to suspect that the aperiodic wave in the lower panel of figure 2.15 is not just due to plosion noise.

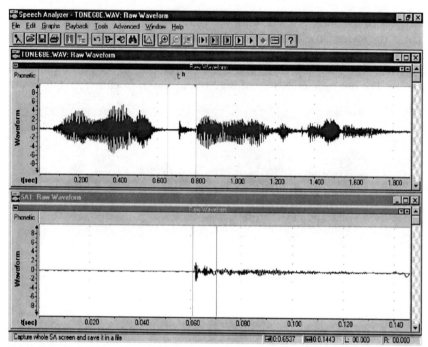

Figure 2.15. Kalam Kohistani utterance, with enlargement of the voiceless aspirated plosive [tʰ].

As a matter of fact, there *is* a burst in the case of the aspirated plosive. Its position is indicated in the lower panel of figure 2.15 by means of two vertical lines. Its duration in this example is a mere 10 ms. The plosion noise corresponding to this burst is produced behind the teeth at the time of the release of the plosive. Following the burst, there is a random wave which continues until the start of the vowel. This random wave represents a whispery sound that is produced at the glottis. When we listen to the whisper in isolation from the rest of the utterance, we hear that it has a quality which is similar to that of the following vowel [u].

2.3.5 Voiceless fricatives

An example of a voiceless fricative was already seen above in figure 2.9. Another example is presented in figure 2.16, namely the voiceless lateral fricative [ɬ] as spoken in Kalam Kohistani [ĩː paɬ] 'this leaf' ('this is a leaf').

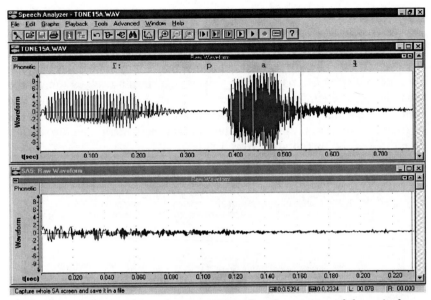

Figure 2.16. Kalam Kohistani utterance, with enlargement of the voiceless lateral fricative [ɬ].

Here, too, the voiceless fricative is characterized by a random wave. The overall amplitude of the wave is clearly smaller than that of the preceding vowel [a]. In figure 2.16, the fricative is located at the end of the utterance. It is quite long in duration (230 ms), which is consistent with the fact that often the last few sounds before a pause are prolonged. It can also be seen how the amplitude of the fricative falls away gradually, which is a typical utterance-final phenomenon as well.

2.3.6 Voiced fricatives

An example of a voiced fricative was shown in figure 2.11 above. Its wave can be described as random, rapid fluctuations superimposed on a periodic wave. The periodic wave corresponds to the buzzing sound that is produced by the vibrating vocal folds. The superimposed random wave corresponds to the friction noise that is produced at the place in the mouth where the articulators approach one another.

2.3.7 Nasals

Nasal consonants show a periodic wave pattern that is quite similar to that of vowels. It was already pointed out above that it may sometimes be quite difficult to distinguish nasals from vowels in a speech wave graph. In the example presented in figure 2.17, involving Kalam Kohistani [ī: manu[ʂ] 'this man' ('this is a man'), both the [m] and the [n] can be distinguished from the surrounding vowels on the basis of the fact that their amplitudes are smaller than those of the surrounding vowels.

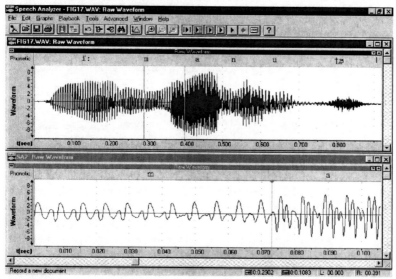

Figure 2.17. Kalam Kohistani utterance, with enlargement of a section of the nasal consonant [m] and the following vowel [a].

A portion of the [m] is enlarged in the lower panel in figure 2.17, together with a portion of the following vowel [a]. Both sounds have a periodic wave structure. However, the wave structure of the nasal is smooth as compared to the wave structure of the vowel, which is more jagged.

2.3.8 Other sonorants

Figures 2.18 and 2.19 present examples of the voiced semivowel [j] and the voiced lateral approximant [l], respectively, as seen in the Kalam Kohistani utterance [aːska jɑl mana] 'to-this mill they-say' ('this is called a mill'). Like nasals, these sounds have a periodic wave type that may be difficult to distinguish from surrounding vowels. In this example, the [j] and [l] have somewhat smaller amplitudes than the neighboring vowels. Also in this example, the [l] has an amplitude which is somewhat smaller than that of the following nasal [m].

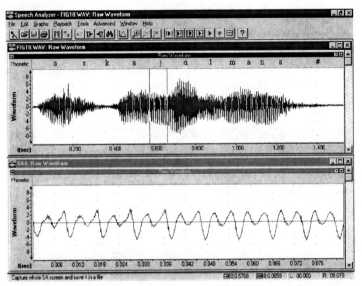

Figure 2.18. Kalam Kohistani utterance, with enlargement of the semivowel [j].

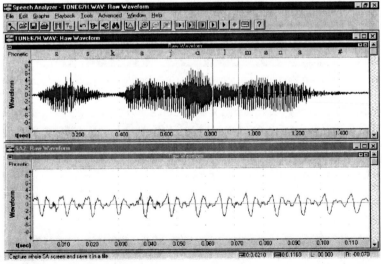

Figure 2.19. Kalam Kohistani utterance, with enlargement of the lateral approximant [l].

Figure 2.20 presents an example of a short trilled [r], taken from the same utterance as shown in figure 2.12. In this example, the duration of the [r] is 82 ms. An enlargement of the [r] is presented in the lower panel. In the middle of the sound, we see a succession of five wave cycles with a medium amplitude. Both at the beginning and the end, the [r] is connected with neighboring sounds through a few vibrations of relatively small amplitude. These are the points in time where the tongue taps rapidly against the roof of the mouth. These taps do not effect a complete closure of the vocal tract, but they do reduce the amplitude of the signal for a short while.

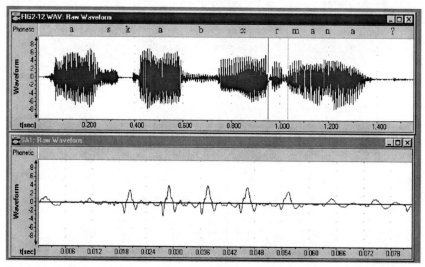

Figure 2.20. Kalam Kohistani utterance, with enlargement of the voiced trill [r].

Figure 2.21 shows the difference between a short [r] and a longer [rː]. The utterance spoken first is [ara], with the shorter trill, while the second utterance following within the same graph is [arːa], with a somewhat exaggerated trill. Both were spoken by the author. The shorter version consists of two taps, the longer version consists of seven taps.

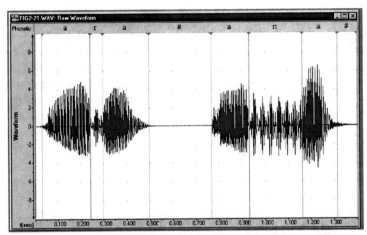

Figure 2.21. [ara] with short trill preceding [aːa] with long trill.

2.3.9 Glottal fricative

Figure 2.22 presents an example of a voiceless glottal fricative [h]. The utterance is [ĩː miːʃ maka hal paʃɑn] 'this man to-me plough is-showing' ('this man is showing me a plough'). The lower panel in figure 2.22 is an enlargement of the [h] together with its neighboring vowels.

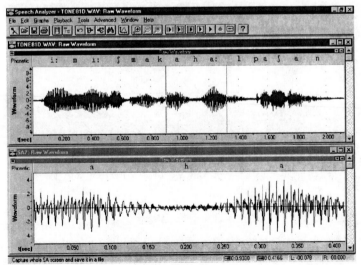

Figure 2.22. Kalam Kohistani utterance, with enlargement of the glottal fricative [h] and its surrounding vowels.

The [h] has an amplitude which is relatively small as compared to the surrounding vowels. There is a gradual decrease of amplitude going from the preceding vowel to the [h], and a gradual increase as we go from the [h] to the following vowel. The wave associated with the voiceless fricative is pretty much random, but someone with a sharp eye may discern some continuing periodicity. Probably, the vocal folds were not vibrating anymore as they were during the production of the preceding vowel, but they may still have been making "swinging" movements that have been affecting the air stream in a regular, periodic manner.

2.3.10 Creaky-voiced vowel

Figure 2.23 presents a speech wave of the Kalam Kohistani utterance [ĩː baːl] 'this hair' ('this is hair'), where the second half of the vowel [aː] is creaky-voiced (laryngealized). The lower panel shows an enlargement of the creaky-voiced part of the vowel. The most noticeable characteristic of creaky voice, in this example, is that the wave resembles a normal periodic wave as seen for a regularly-voiced vowel, but the cycle period appears to double at some point, and at the end of this example even appears to triple.

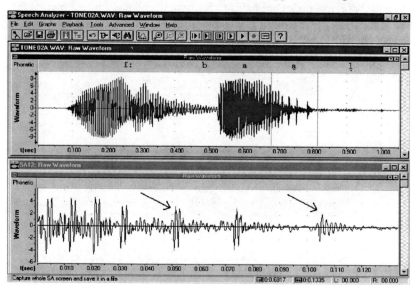

Figure 2.23. Kalam Kohistani utterance, with creaky-voiced vowel.

As in normal voicing, the periodic nature of the wave is due to the opening and closing movements of the vocal folds. Each time the vocal folds close (in any voiced sound), the flow of air is suddenly interrupted. This sudden interruption of airflow disturbs the air pressure directly above the larynx, setting off major vibrations. Such a disturbance is called a pulse, and in a stretch of voiced speech there are as many pulses as there are cycles in the speech wave.

The characteristic feature of creaky voice is that at some points pulses are skipped. In figure 2.23, the first arrow points to a major peak in the speech wave that corresponds to such a voicing pulse. It can be seen that the distance to the preceding major peak is twice as long as compared to the distance between major peaks in the first three periods of the wave. The vocal folds have skipped one pulse, so to speak. At the place of the second arrow, they have skipped even two pulses.

2.4 Determining segment boundaries

2.4.1 Purpose

In traditional phonetic transcription, we describe an utterance as a string of discrete consonant and vowel sounds (segments). Actual speech, of course, does not consist of discrete elements, put one after another. It takes time for the articulators (tongue, lips, jaw, and so forth) to move from one position to another. Normally, as soon as the articulators have come close enough to the target positions for one sound, they already start moving to assume the target positions for the next sound. As the articulators move from one position to the next, the sound that is produced changes gradually.

In view of this continuous nature of speaking and speech sound, Shoup and Pfeifer (1976:204) write:

> It could be argued that there is no boundary point between adjacent sounds, but rather a boundary region in which the transition from one sound to the next takes place. This region can have the characteristics of one or both of the sounds it separates, and it may carry information regarding the identity of neighboring sounds.

While it is often more accurate to speak of boundary regions between adjacent sounds, rather than boundary points, it is more practical in many situations to simply determine boundary points.

The need to determine segment boundaries at all, and the precision with which this needs to be done, depends on the problem that one is trying to solve. In many cases, where one would like to study the output of acoustic analysis, or where one includes a graph in a lecture or a publication, it is helpful if that graph is roughly divided into consonant and vowel segments, and if the boundary lines and the phonetic transcription of these segments are included in the graph. This reminds the researcher and his or her audience of what is represented in the graph, and of what part of the graph corresponds to what part of the utterance under study. If this is the only purpose of determining segment boundaries, then the exact locations of the boundaries do not matter that much, as long as they are roughly correct.

A more precise determination of segment boundaries is important in all cases where durations play an important role. It may be the case that durations are the primary focus of research (for instance, one may be studying the phonetic characteristics of contrastive long and short segments, or one may be studying processes of lengthening or shortening). It may also be that one needs to know how certain features of speech are aligned in time with other features. For instance, one may need to know if a relatively high pitch level is reached early or late in the vowel. In such cases, one needs to measure time from the beginning of the vowel. In other words, one needs to determine where that vowel starts.

Some researchers are interested in building a computer database where acoustic data (perhaps even video data) for a language are stored along with a phonetic and linguistic analysis of that data. Such a project is normally undertaken for the benefit of future researchers, who will perhaps approach such a database with research questions that cannot be foreseen at the time of the creation of the database. In such a project, it is important that segmentation be done in a precise, consistent manner. For the sake of future researchers, the criteria for determining segment boundaries need to be made explicit, so as to help them understand to what extent they can rely on these boundaries as they carry out their research.

2.4.2 Guidelines

The following notes are based on a set of segmentation guidelines that were developed for a Dutch acoustic database project (van Zanten, Damen, and van Houten 1991:17ff.). These may not be relevant in all cases. However, particularly if there is any chance that segment durations will be a primary or subsidiary focus of study, then segmentation should be based on criteria that are as complete and explicit as possible. (The researcher may have to add language-specific criteria to the general criteria that are mentioned here.)

Listening is a very helpful technique for the determination of rough segment boundaries. In good software packages for acoustic speech analysis, one can position a cursor somewhere in an utterance and listen to the part of the utterance to the left of the cursor, and the part to the right of the cursor. In this way, one can try to determine by ear where one segment ends and the next one starts. However, when precision and consistency in segmentation are required, the final decision on segment boundaries should be based on formal, visual criteria, rather than on auditory criteria, because another listener might not hear the sound in the same way as the analyst.

In cases where a researcher is planning to carry out manipulation of the speech wave itself, special care needs to be taken as to where segment boundaries are placed. Such manipulation may involve changing the duration or the amplitude of certain sounds in an utterance. It may also involve "splicing," where a segment or a longer portion of an utterance is replaced with a portion taken from another utterance. In such and similar cases, manipulation can result in discontinuities in the speech wave at the boundaries of the involved segments. Such discontinuities can sometimes be heard as popping noises and may negatively affect the quality of the resulting speech.

In cases where manipulation is planned, then, segment boundaries should be positioned as much as possible at positive zero crossings. Zero crossings are points where the speech wave curve crosses the zero line (the horizontal line representing average air pressure). Positive zero crossings are crossings where the curve is rising: it comes from below and goes up. (One may just as well position all boundaries at negative zero crossings, as long as one is consistent: either all boundaries at positive crossings, or at negative crossings). An example of a segment boundary positioned at a positive zero crossing is given in figure 2.24.

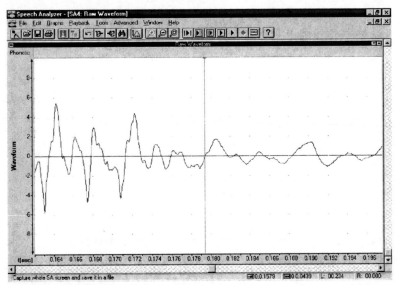

Figure 2.24. Segment boundary (vertical line) positioned at a positive zero crossing.

If manipulation of the speech wave is not planned, then it may be better not to bother with positive zero crossings.

In many cases, a significant amplitude difference between two successive cycles in a speech wave is a good cue for segment boundaries. In fact, a sudden change in overall amplitude is often a better criterion than a change in the finer structure of the speech wave.

If the change in amplitude, going from one sound to the following sound, is gradual rather than abrupt, or if there is no significant amplitude change at all, then a change in the structure (the finer pattern of fluctuations) of wave cycles may be used as a boundary cue.

If neither amplitude nor wave structure provide a clear criterion, then a segment boundary should be arbitrarily positioned in the middle of the transitional region between one sound and the next. Often the transitional region can be demarcated on the basis of amplitude. A transition starts where the amplitude begins to increase (or decrease) consistently with each following successive wave cycle, and ends where the amplitude does not significantly increase (or decrease) any further. See figure 2.25 for an example.

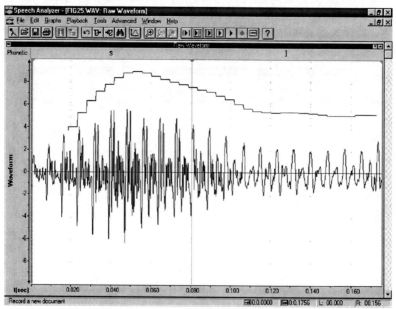

Figure 2.25. Segment boundary placed in the middle of the transitional region between the [3] and [l]; the transition was taken as the region of gradually decreasing amplitude, shown in the signal amplitude curve plotted above the speech wave.

Before silence it may be difficult to determine where a vowel or another sonorant sound ends. A guideline here is that the vowel or sonorant consonant ends at the point where the wave structure as it is seen in the louder portions of that sound, can no longer clearly be recognized. Often some minor ripples may still be seen after that point, sometimes a bit of weak noise (random wave with a small amplitude). If the following sound is a plosive, then these ripples or weak noise are to be taken as part of the silent interval of that following plosive. Figure 2.26 presents an example of a boundary between the vowel [oᵘ] and the voiceless plosive [t], as spoken in the word *boat*. Some relatively small vibrations are still seen directly to the right of the boundary. However, the size of these vibrations is significantly smaller than that of the wave cycles seen to the left of the boundary, and their shape, too, no longer clearly resembles that of the preceding cycles. Consequently, the ripples seen directly to the right of the boundary line are included as a part of the silent interval of the [t].

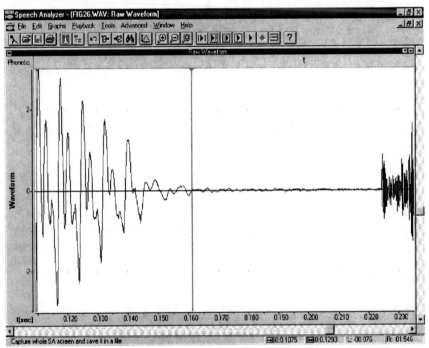

Figure 2.26. Determining the end point of a vowel before (near-) silence.

Fricatives are supposed to start from the point where a random wave structure is visible (this random wave may be superimposed on a periodic wave if there is voicing as well). Fricatives end at the point where the random wave structure disappears. Figure 2.27 illustrates a boundary between the vowel [a] and the voiced fricative [z], taken from the Kalam Kohistani word [nazɔːr] 'nose'.

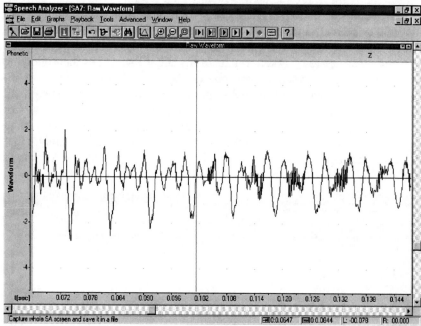

Figure 2.27. Boundary between vowel and voiced fricative [z].

Burst waves, such as those seen in plosives, have very short durations. Particularly in cases where burst durations are an object of research, it is important to determine the boundaries of the burst as precisely as possible. In such circumstances, one may have to relax the principle of positive zero crossings, if one is following it. An example of this is seen in figure 2.28, involving the boundary between the noise burst of a [t] and a following vowel in the Dutch word *auto* 'car'.

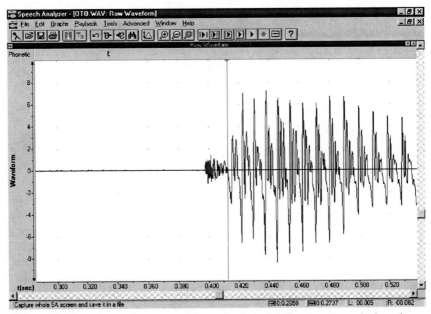

Figure 2.28. Boundary between burst of [t] and following vowel placed at a negative zero crossing.

Different languages have different inventories of sounds and different possible combinations of sounds. Therefore, the challenges posed by one language for the task of determining segment boundaries may be different from those posed by another language. Detailed segmentation criteria will to a certain extent be unique for one language, and will need to be developed and made explicit as a researcher gains experience in segmenting words and sentences uttered in that language.

3

Sound Spectrograms and Spectra

The speech wave graphs (speech waveforms, oscillograms) that were discussed in chapter 2 provide one way of looking at speech. Speech waveforms are direct representations of air pressure fluctuations; their production does not require any further analysis of the speech signal.

Speech waveforms already provide a lot of information about speech. Inspection of waveforms can give clues about phonetic features of segments (consonants and vowels), about their relative loudness, and about their duration. However, other views of a speech signal are possible that provide additional information.

The development of the sound spectrograph, in the early 1940s, has meant a tremendous boost for the science of phonetics. The sound spectrograms (also called sonagrams) that are produced by this machine provide a wealth of information about the acoustic properties of sounds in general and speech sounds in particular. In the early days, some researchers believed that it would be possible to teach a wide range of people to "read" spectrograms of spoken utterances (that is, to recover the original, spoken message by mere visual inspection of its spectrogram). For a short while it was hoped that this could be a solution for the communication problems of deaf people (see Potter, Kopp, and Green 1947).

While this hope proved to be too optimistic, it is still true that the spectrograph has played an essential role in the rapid advancement of the field of phonetics after the Second World War. Spectrograms are particularly useful for studying the acoustic properties of individual vowels and consonants. They show, for example, the differences between vowel qualities such as [i], [a], and [u] much more clearly than speech wave graphs (in fact it is often very difficult, if not impossible, to recognize vowel qualities in speech wave graphs, even for experienced phoneticians).

The spectrograph as a stand-alone piece of equipment has become obsolete. As one phonetician wrote some forty years ago: "…it will eventually be old fashioned to build speech processing devices for specific purposes. Instead, the phonetics laboratory computer will be equipped with programs for simulating any desired form of speech analysis and synthesis" (Fant 1968:175). Today, even a standard personal computer can be equipped with such programs.

In this chapter we will first look at what spectrograms are. Following that, we will discuss a number of acoustic features that are seen in spectrograms and that are particularly relevant to the study of speech sounds. Finally, we will look more closely at some classes of speech sounds and what can be learned about them from spectrograms.

At various points we will also be looking at spectra. While spectrograms have a time dimension (they show how acoustic parameters change over time), a spectrum presents a snapshot taken at a single moment. Spectra are helpful when more precise measurements need to be taken at a certain point in an utterance.

3.1 Sound spectrograms: Time, frequency, and intensity

3.1.1 Sine waves and complex waves

A perfectly simple and smooth wave is called a SINE WAVE. An example of a sine wave is presented in figure 3.1.

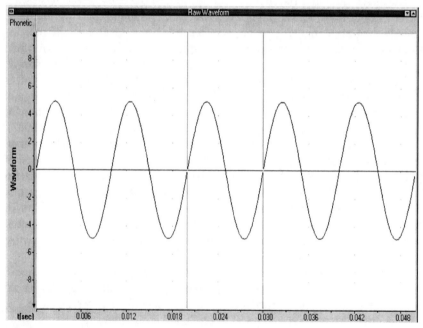

Figure 3.1. A sine wave with a cycle period of 10 ms (vertical lines demarcate one cycle).

Sine waves have a simple rising and falling pattern that is repeated over and over. One such repetition is called a cycle, and the duration of one cycle is called the cycle period. The sine wave shown in figure 3.1 has a cycle period of 10 ms (millisecond, a thousandth of a second). As 100 periods of 10 ms would fit into one second, we say that the wave has a frequency of 100 Hz (hertz, "cycles per second").

Another sine wave is shown in figure 3.2. This sine wave has a frequency of 1,000 Hz and an amplitude (magnitude of the vibrations) which is half the amplitude of the wave in figure 3.1.

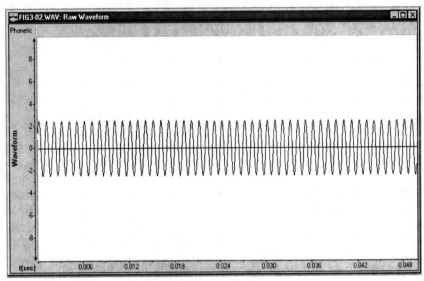

Figure 3.2. Sine wave with a frequency of 1000 Hz.

When a sine wave is played over a loudspeaker, we hear a so-called pure tone. The 100 Hz sine wave of figure 3.1 will produce a relatively low tone; the 1,000 Hz wave will produce a much higher tone.

It is possible to combine two sine waves into one single wave by simple addition. At any point in time, the deviation from zero of the resulting complex wave is equal to the sum of the deviations of the sine waves at that point. Figure 3.3 shows the result of adding the two sine waves presented above.

In the example, there are two sine waves of 100 and 1,000 Hz; the greatest common denominator of these two numbers is 100.)

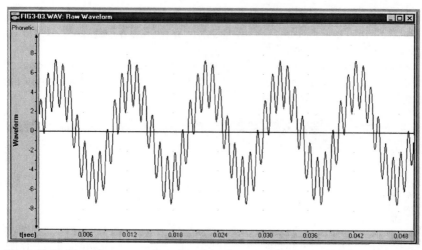

Figure 3.3. Complex wave representing the combination of two sine waves 100 Hz and 1000 Hz, respectively.

In the wave pattern of figure 3.3, the original sine waves can still be recognized (the vibrations that belong to the higher-frequency wave are superimposed on the lower-frequency wave). The complex wave itself has a cycle period of 10 ms (the complex pattern is repeated every 10 ms), equaling a frequency of 100 Hz. This frequency is called the fundamental frequency of the complex wave. Fundamental frequency corresponds to the pitch of a sound as we hear it. (In general, the fundamental frequency of a complex periodic wave is equal to the greatest common denominator of the frequencies of its constituent sine waves.)

Figure 3.4 presents a complex wave that is the result of the addition of three sine waves, namely of 100, 200, and 300 Hz. This wave, too, shows a regular pattern that recurs every 10 ms, equaling a fundamental frequency of 100 Hz. (Note that the pattern here is different from that in the previous figure: the original frequencies are not seen as one riding on top of the other.)

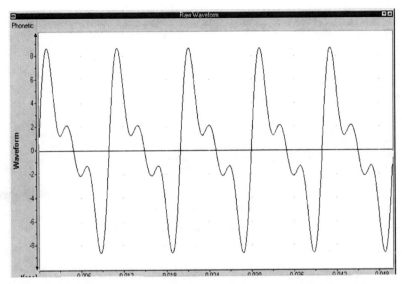

Figure 3.4. Complex wave representing the combination of three sine waves of 100, 200, and 300 Hz, respectively.

3.1.2 Spectral analysis

Thus far we have been creating complex waves by taking simple sine waves of different frequencies and amplitudes, and adding them together. The opposite process is to take a complex wave and analyse it into its component sine waves. For instance, we could take the wave in figure 3.3 and determine (for example, by means of some mathematical procedure) that it is the result of adding together two sine waves of 100 and 1,000 Hz. We say that the complex wave can be analysed (decomposed) into two sine wave components (also called FREQUENCY COMPONENTS, or simply components), one of 100 Hz and one of 1,000 Hz.

Now, the basic assumption of SPECTRAL ANALYSIS is that every complex sound can be decomposed into a set of simple sine waves with different frequencies and amplitudes. In other words, a complex wave can always be thought of as the sum of a number of simple sine waves.

An example of spectral analysis carried out by computer is seen in figure 3.5. Input to the analysis is the complex wave from figure 3.4. As was explained above, that wave was the result of adding together sine waves with frequencies of 100, 200, and 300 Hz.

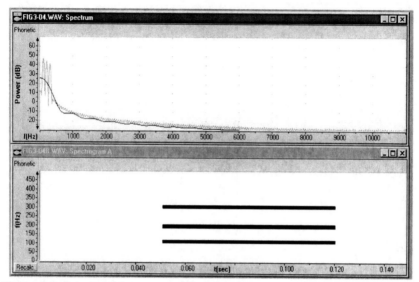

Figure 3.5. Spectrum (upper panel) and spectrogram of the wave shown in figure 3.4.

The upper panel presents a SPECTRUM (frequency along the horizontal axis, amplitude along the vertical axis). Indeed, when we look at the trace of the spectrum analyser, we see three sharp peaks on the left side that indicate the presence of sine wave components at 100, 200, and 300 Hz.

The lower panel in figure 3.5 presents a (narrow-band) spectrogram (time along the horizontal axis, frequency along the vertical axis, amplitude represented by degrees of darkness). We see three horizontal dark lines, which again correspond to the three sine wave components out of which the complex wave was built up.

As was said, the horizontal dimension in a spectrogram (as in the lower panel of figure 3.5) represents time, just as in waveforms. The vertical dimension in a spectrogram represents frequency. In order to produce a spectrogram, a computer "looks" at a sound signal at successive moments of time and determines what frequencies are present in the signal at each moment. In other words: it performs a series of spectral analyses, starting at the beginning of a sound signal and continuing until the end of the signal. If a component of a certain frequency is found at a certain point in time, then a dot will be plotted in the spectrogram at the intersection of the frequency of the component and the point in time where it was found.

The sound signal in figure 3.5 is completely stationary: it does not change at all over time. Therefore, at successive points in time exactly the same frequency components are found. This state of affairs is responsible for the three unchanging straight horizontal lines that are seen in the spectrogram in the lower panel.

The darkness of different areas in a spectrogram corresponds to the amplitude of the components that are represented at those areas. When components are strong (they have a relatively large amplitude, or, to use another term, a relatively large intensity), they will be seen as having a higher degree of darkness. When components are weak, they will be lighter. These different degrees of intensity do not show up in figure 3.5, but they do show up in the spectrograms presented below. (Amplitude is a term that refers to the magnitude of air pressure fluctuations, while intensity refers to the energy that is expended in bringing these fluctuations about. The two are directly related: the intensity of a sound wave is proportional to the square of its amplitude.)

3.1.3 Broad-band and narrow-band spectrograms

The information presented in spectrograms is not always as precise as we would like. In all three dimensions: time, frequency, and intensity, values within a certain range are lumped together during analysis. In this subsection we will focus on time and frequency. (In the dimension of intensity, we normally do not need to discriminate between a great number of different values.)

First of all, it must be understood that we cannot extract frequency components from a complex wave if we look at too small a section of the wave. The pattern of fluctuations that characterizes a speech wave unfolds itself over a certain period of time. Therefore, we must look at a section of the speech wave that is large enough so that the complete fluctuation pattern can be seen. In the case of a periodic wave, this means that we must look at least at one complete cycle of the wave. If we look at a portion of the wave that is smaller than one cycle, we are bound to make mistakes, because we are not looking at the whole pattern.

Spectrographic analysis, then, always involves a so-called time window, which is the portion of a speech wave that is being inspected at one time for the sake of finding frequency components. During analysis, this time window "slides" through the speech wave from beginning to end.

If the time window is wider, then a larger section of the speech wave is inspected at one time and the analysis is based on more data. As a result, finer distinctions can be made in the frequency dimension. However, the disadvantage of a wider time window is that events that occur close together in time become blurred in the spectrogram. For instance, if a window of 100 ms is used, one might not be able to distinguish events that occur less than 100 ms after one another. An example of such events are the pulses of energy that are due to the vibrating movements of the vocal folds. These pulses may occur 10 or 5 ms, or even less, after one another. If the time window has a width of 100 ms, then certainly voicing pulses will not be seen as separate events in the spectrogram.

On the other hand, if we use a smaller time window it becomes more difficult to separate different frequency components. For instance, we can choose a time window that will allow voicing pulses to show up as separate events in the time dimension, but then we might not be able to distinguish components that are less than, say, 300 Hz apart from one another in the frequency dimension. What we see, then, is that there is a trade-off in spectrographic analysis: A higher resolution in the frequency dimension brings along a lower resolution in the time dimension. Conversely, a higher resolution in the time dimension brings along a lower resolution in the frequency dimension.

The old spectrograph came with two standard analysis settings. One is called narrow-band analysis, where the word narrow refers to the dimension of frequency. A narrow-band spectrogram makes finer (narrower) distinctions in frequency but coarser distinctions in time. The other setting is called broad-band analysis (or wide-band analysis). A broad-band spectrogram makes coarser (broader) distinctions in frequency and finer distinctions in time. Current computer programs sometimes still offer these two standard options, while at the same time allowing a range of other analysis settings. (Narrow-band analysis corresponds to a frequency bandwidth of approximately 45 Hz and a window of about 100 ms. Broad-band analysis corresponds to a bandwidth of some 300 Hz and a window of about 5 ms.) The choice between these settings (narrow-band, broad-band, or something else) is determined by the problem one is trying to solve.

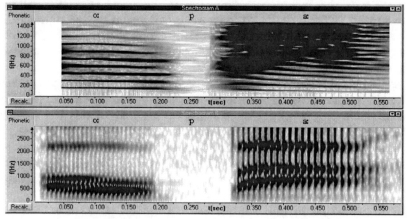

Figure 3.6. Narrow-band spectrogram (upper panel) and broad-band spectrogram of Dutch *opa* 'granddad'.

A narrow-band spectrogram

The upper panel in figure 3.6 shows a narrow-band spectrogram. The frequency range displayed along the vertical axis is 0–1,500 Hz. We can clearly see the separate harmonics as horizontal, black lines running from left to right through the spectrogram. HARMONICS are sine wave components of periodic sound signals. They are evenly spaced in the frequency dimension. If the lowest harmonic (the fundamental) has a frequency of 150 Hz, then the second harmonic will occur at 300 Hz, the third at 450 Hz, the fourth at 600 Hz, and so on. This situation is roughly the case during the first part of the example. Near the end of the example, the lowest harmonic occurs at approximately 90 Hz, and further harmonics at 180 Hz, 270 Hz, 360 Hz, and so forth. (See section 3.2.4 for further discussion of harmonics.)

While there is good frequency resolution in the narrow-band spectrogram, allowing us to distinguish components that are as close together as 90 Hz, the representation along the horizontal axis (time) is blurred. The boundaries of the plosive [p], for instance, cannot be located in this figure; rather, the harmonics of the preceding vowel seem to continue into the consonant, and the harmonics of the following vowel seem to start before the end of the consonant. The plosive, of course, consists of a period of silence followed by a noise burst, and does not have a harmonic structure of itself. Due to the wide setting of the time window, information belonging to one segment has been merged with information belonging to a neighbouring segment, and the boundaries between the segments are not clearly visible anymore.

A broad-band spectrogram

In the broad-band spectrogram presented in the lower panel of figure 3.6 (the frequency range displayed is 0–3000 Hz), we see the opposite state of affairs. Due to a lack of frequency resolution, separate harmonics cannot be distinguished in this picture. The dark bands seen in the picture are not harmonics, but formants (resonances in the vocal tract, see section 3.2.5). On the other hand, we can take a good look at the timing of events. The boundaries between the two vowels and the consonant can be seen (the formants belong to the vowels; the middle section without formants belongs to the plosive). Furthermore, we are able to discern the individual voicing pulses; they are seen as vertical dark lines that occur one after another during the vowels. No pulses are seen during the [p], which is voiceless.

For most practical purposes, a speech researcher will inspect broad-band rather than narrow-band spectrograms. One reason is that the interest of the researcher is often in the formants, rather than in the separate harmonics. The detection of formants is actually facilitated by the blurring of information in the dimension of frequency. Another reason is that one often wants to see with some accuracy how acoustic parameters change over time, and for this purpose a good resolution in the time domain is required.

3.1.4 Spectra

A spectrum is a two-dimensional representation, with frequency displayed along the horizontal axis, and intensity along the vertical axis. A spectrum shows for a section of a sound wave what frequency components are present and what the relative intensities (strengths) of these components are. While a spectrogram gives a dynamic picture of a stretch of sound (it shows how acoustic parameters change over time), a spectrum gives a static picture: it has no time dimension.

As with spectrograms, the appearance of a spectrum depends to an important extent on the size of the time window that is chosen for analysis. If a wave is periodic and the analysis window is smaller than the size of one cycle of the wave, then the analysis will be based on incomplete information. For the sake of precision, one would like to calculate a spectrum over as large a stretch of sound as possible. However, if one is interested in the spectral properties of only one vowel or consonant, one is constrained by the duration of that vowel or consonant. In fact, one will often be confined to a section in the middle of a segment, where the sound is maximally stationary, as the peripheral regions of speech sounds are often heavily influenced by neighboring sounds.

Figure 3.7 gives a spectrum of the wave displayed in figure 3.3. Two sharp peaks are seen, that correspond to the two component frequencies at 100 and 1,000 Hz.

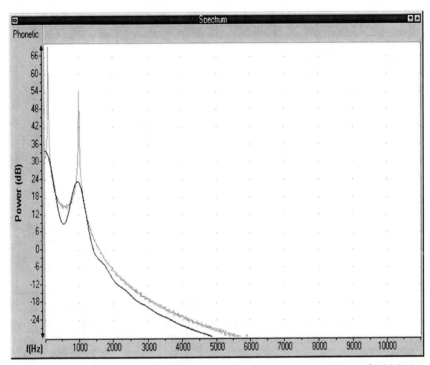

Figure 3.7. Spectrum showing frequency components at 100 Hz and 1000 Hz.

Figure 3.8 presents a spectrum taken in the middle of the vowel [a:] of Dutch *opa* 'granddad'. The duration of the analysed portion of the speech wave was 9 ms; it included exactly one cycle period.

The many little peaks seen in this spectrum correspond to the individual harmonics. They are spaced approximately 110 Hz apart. The intensity of these little peaks fluctuates. The general trend is that they are higher in the left part of the figure and lower in the right part. In other words, the lower frequency components are stronger than the higher frequency components. Furthermore, we see that some peaks stand out as stronger than other peaks in their vicinity. At approximately 800 Hz, 1,400 Hz, and 2,300 Hz we see the highest peaks in this spectrum (marked in the figure by little arrowheads). These highest peaks correspond to the dark bands seen in the lower panel of figure 3.6. They are due to resonances in the vocal tract (formants; section 3.2.5).

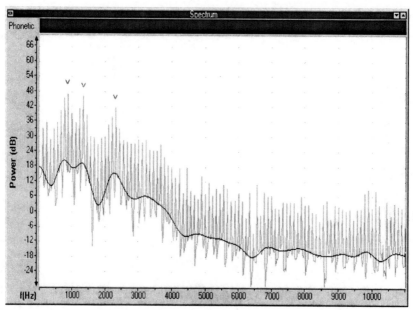

Figure 3.8. Spectrum taken in the middle of the vowel [aː] of Dutch 'granddad'; arrow heads mark the three highest peaks.

3.2 Basic acoustic properties of speech signals

We will now discuss a number of basic properties of speech sound as seen in spectrograms:

1. overall gap
2. continuous energy
3. periodicity
4. harmonic structure
5. formants
6. anti-formants

In what follows, it will sometimes be convenient to use the term *energy* as in "there is a concentration of energy in the higher frequency ranges," which means the components in the higher frequencies have a relatively strong intensity.

3.2.1 Overall gap

An overall gap in the spectrogram is seen at places that are associated with (near-) silence. In theory, no energy (grey spots or grey regions) should be seen at all during silent periods. Where there is no sound, there can be no frequency components. Often, however, one will see some energy even during silent periods. This can be due to echo or background noise in the recording. Some noise might also be introduced by the recording equipment and by the speech processing software. Some speech processing software amplifies high frequency components. If there is background noise in the high frequencies, the software will also amplify the background noise. Often, then, there will be spurious noise resulting in some background shading of spectrograms, which a researcher will have to see through.

At the place of an overall gap in the spectrogram, no significant acoustic phonetic parameters can be measured. What can be measured, of course, is the duration of the gap. Figure 3.9 presents a broad-band spectrogram of Dutch *opa* 'granddad'. Phonetic transcriptions of the three segments are provided in the bar directly above the spectrogram.

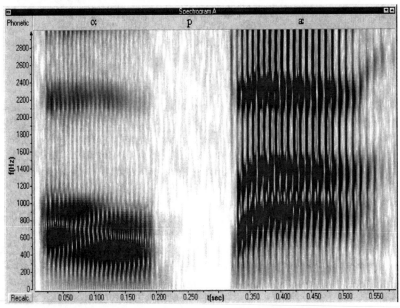

Figure 3.9. Broad-band spectrogram of Dutch *opa* 'granddad'.

A gap is seen in the middle of this spectrogram that corresponds to the silent interval of the voiceless plosive [p]. Some spurious energy is present in the gap that might be due to one or another of the reasons mentioned above. (Someone with a sharp eye will see a continuation of the fundamental frequency and the lower two formants of the [o:] during the first part of the [p]. This is due to vocal fold vibration continuing for a short while—some 30 ms—after the lips are closed to form the occlusive.)

3.2.2 Continuous energy

Our discussion, thus far, of spectral analysis has ignored the case of random speech waves. We have seen how sine waves can be added together to produce a complex wave. In the examples, this addition resulted in a wave that was itself periodic, showing a complex but repetitive pattern. It was stated that the complex waves, in turn, can be analysed in order to extract their component sine waves. However, a random wave has no repetitive structure (there seems to be no regularity). So how can component sine waves be extracted from a random wave?

The answer is that random waves are composed of an infinite number of sine waves, whose frequencies form a continuum. While for periodic sound waves we will find one component at, say, 100 Hz, the next one at 200 Hz, the third one at 300 Hz, and so on, random waves are associated with an infinite number of components between any two points on the frequency scale. Since each component of a sound wave contains energy (in the form of vibrating air—larger vibrations contain more energy, smaller vibrations contain less energy), we say that random sound waves are characterized by a continuous distribution of energy along the frequency scale.

This continuous distribution of energy is not necessarily uniform. Sounds that are associated with random waves are distinguished from one another in that one sound will show a concentration of energy within one range of the frequency spectrum, say between 2,000 Hz and 4,000 Hz, while another sound will show a concentration within another frequency range, say between 500 Hz and 1,500 Hz.

Figure 3.10 presents a broad-band spectrogram of the word *say* taken out of the utterance *Say boat again.* The frequency range displayed is 0–11,000 Hz. The differences between the voiceless fricative [s] and the following ized vowel [eⁱ] are easy to see. The vowel is characterized by the vertical striation associated with voicing pulses, and by the more-or-less horizontal bands that correspond to formants. The fricative, on the other hand, is seen as a cloud of energy without much structure. The energy concentration starts at around 3,000 Hz and spreads upward into the higher frequencies.

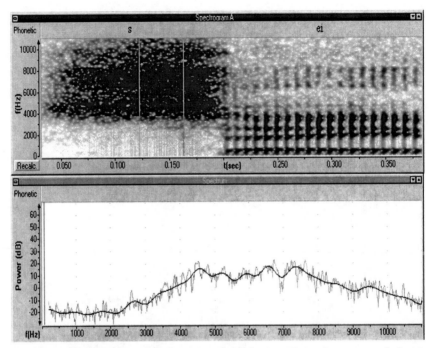

Figure 3.10. Spectrogram (upper panel) of the word *say;* lower panel shows a spectrum calculated over a 40 ms section of the [s].

A spectrum of the [s] is shown in the lower panel of figure 3.10. This spectrum was calculated over a 40 ms section somewhere in the middle of the fricative. The spectrum shows that there is relatively little energy in the band of 0–2,500 Hz. From there we see increasing energy. The greatest amount of energy is seen in the band of 4,500–7,500 Hz. For the frequencies above 7,500 Hz, we see a gradually decreasing level of energy.

Continuous energy (with a concentration in one or another range of the frequency spectrum) is associated with the random waves of fricatives and the bursts of plosives.

3.2.3 Periodicity

Periodic speech waves are repetitive: (approximately) the same wave pattern is repeated every so many milliseconds. The amount of time needed for one cycle is called the period of the speech wave. Random waves are aperiodic: they are not repetitive and, hence, there is no cycle period. Periodicity in speech is normally due to the vibration (repeated opening and closing) of the vocal folds.

Sound Spectrograms and Spectra

Periodicity shows up in spectrograms in different ways. In broad-band spectrograms, the energy pulses that are associated with the vocal fold vibrations are seen as separate events (vertical dark lines). For an example, see figure 3.11, representing a broad-band spectrogram of the entire sentence *Say boat again.*

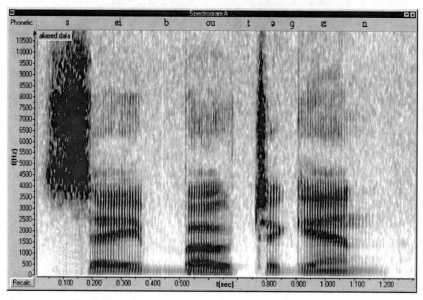

Figure 3.11. Broad-band spectrogram of *Say boat again.*

The frequency range displayed is 0–11,000 Hz. Phonetic transcriptions are provided in the bar directly above the spectrogram. Phonetic symbols are centered above the sections in the spectrogram to which they belong. The reader should first inspect the sections that correspond to the vowel sounds. Their vertically striated patterns are clearly noticeable. Next look at the [n], which is the final sound of this utterance. In this example, the [n] has a relatively low overall energy and, as a consequence, the striation pattern is not as clear as with the vowels. However, it can still be seen in the [n], particularly in the lower frequency ranges.

It is instructive to note that it is possible to determine the fundamental frequency of the speech signal in the striated areas: the distance from one voicing pulse to the next is equal to the cycle period. If the cycle period is measured in milliseconds, then one should divide 1,000 by the cycle period to arrive at the fundamental frequency expressed in hertz. It may be easier, though, to count the number of pulses within a longer time stretch, for instance 100 ms. This number should be multiplied by 10 (if the time stretch was 100 ms) to arrive at the average fundamental frequency within that time interval.

Children's voices and female voices are normally higher pitched than male voices. During stretches of higher-pitched speech (for instance in the higher pitch ranges of women and children), separate voicing pulses may no longer be seen in spectrograms. The reason is that higher pitch is due to a greater frequency of the voicing pulses. When these pulses occur very close after one another (less than 4 or 3 ms), they will become blurred even in a broad-band spectrogram.

Another indicator of periodicity is the presence of a band of energy near the bottom of the spectrogram (the voice bar). This low-frequency energy band represents the relatively strong fundamental frequency of the signal. Even when higher frequencies are too weak to show up clearly in a spectrogram, the fundamental frequency will normally still be seen. In figure 3.11, look at the voiced plosives [b] and [g]. During these sounds, a grey band runs along the bottom of the spectrogram. This grey band is also seen during the vowels and the final nasal. It is not seen during the initial voiceless fricative [s] Neither is it seen during the release and most of the closure of the voiceless plosive [t]. (It does continue for a brief while into the closure of the [t].)

3.2.4 Harmonic structure

The fundamental frequency of a complex periodic wave is equal to the greatest common denominator of its frequency components. Suppose a signal is composed of three frequencies of 300, 400, and 700 Hz, respectively. The greatest common denominator of these three numbers is 100 (the greatest number by which all three can be divided). The complex wave in this example will have a fundamental frequency of 100 Hz (equaling a cycle period of 10 ms).

The components of periodic waves are often called HARMONICS. A sound with a fully developed harmonic structure has harmonics at the fundamental frequency (for example, 100 Hz) and at all whole-number multiples of the fundamental frequency (200 Hz, 300 Hz, 400 Hz, and so forth, if the fundamental frequency is 100 Hz). The fundamental frequency is called the first harmonic, and the following harmonics are numbered accordingly.

In the case of speech, the sound that is produced by the vibration of the vocal folds has such a fully developed harmonic structure. This harmonic structure often shows up clearly in narrow-band spectrograms. An example is seen in figure 3.12. The lower panel presents a narrow-band spectrogram of the sentence Say boat again. The frequency range displayed is 0–1,500 Hz. During the vowels, the harmonic structure can clearly be seen as a series of horizontal black lines (12 or 13 in number in this example) that correspond to the individual harmonics. They are evenly spaced in the vertical dimension, the first one occurring at the fundamental frequency, the second one at twice the fundamental frequency, the third one at three times the fundamental frequency, and so on.

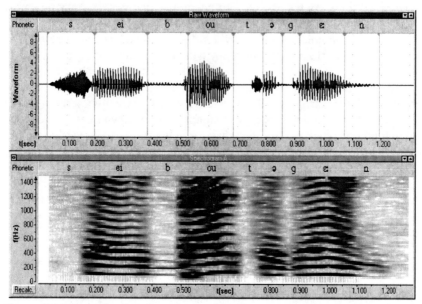

Figure 3.12. Speech wave (upper panel) and narrow-band spectrogram of *Say boat again.*

In the figure, the harmonics are curved in some places. This is due to rises and falls in fundamental frequency. The fundamental frequency of voiced speech is related to the rate of vibration of the vocal folds. A higher rate of vibration results in a higher fundamental frequency (and a higher perceived pitch). A raise in fundamental frequency affects all the harmonics present at that time, as these are located at frequencies that are multiples of the fundamental frequency.

Narrow-band spectrograms provide a way of extracting the fundamental frequency curve of an utterance. In theory, one can look at the first harmonic and measure its frequency at successive points in time. However, the resolution of spectrograms is not good enough to measure the frequency of the first harmonic very precisely. A better way, therefore, is to measure the frequency of, say, the tenth harmonic at successive points in time and divide this number by 10. The frequency of the tenth harmonic is 10 times the frequency of the first harmonic, and a change of 10 Hz in the first harmonic is reflected as a change of 100 Hz in the tenth harmonic. In other words, fluctuations that are difficult to notice in the first harmonic are easier to notice in a much higher harmonic. Nowadays, not many people use this method because of the availability of reasonably performing computer programs for fundamental frequency extraction.

3.2.5 Formants

The source-filter model of speech production

A body of air contained in a cavity has a preferred frequency (called the RESONANCE FREQUENCY). For instance, when we blow over the opening of an empty bottle, we will produce a sound that has a certain pitch. Our blowing generates vibrations of the air inside the bottle, and these vibrations have a fundamental frequency that depends on the size and the shape of the bottle. Generally speaking, if the bottle is long (from top to bottom), it will produce a low-pitched sound. If the bottle is short, it will produce a high-pitched sound.

In speaking, sound generated at the glottis (or at some constriction above the glottis) travels through a number of cavities in the vocal tract. The shape and size of these cavities are variable, depending on the position and shape of the lips, the degree of opening of the mouth, the position and height of the tongue, and so on. These cavities in the vocal tract have their preferred frequencies in the same way that bottles do. When sound travels through these cavities, frequency components that are close to the preferred frequency of a cavity are amplified (they become stronger than the surrounding frequency components). Resonances that are associated with cavities in the vocal tract are called FORMANTS.

Phoneticians often describe speech production as a two-stage process, which they call the SOURCE-FILTER MODEL. The idea is that there is a source that generates sound. This source can be the vibration of the vocal folds, in which case the sound is periodic and has a harmonic structure. Alternatively, the source can be friction or plosion at some point in the vocal tract, in which case the generated sound is aperiodic.

The generation of a source signal is the first stage of speech production. In the second stage, the source signal is passed through a filter that selectively amplifies certain frequencies in the source signal (it can also attenuate certain frequencies, as we will see in section 3.2.6). This filter is, in fact, the vocal tract (or the section of the vocal tract above the source) with its resonance cavities. The vocal tract filter adds different colorings to the source signal, and in this way vowel quality differences (such as between [i], [a], and [u]) are created, to give one example.

Formants (resonances; the term "poles" is also used in some contexts) are the most important aspect of the vocal tract filter. A formant is responsible for the amplification of frequency components that occur in the vicinity of the formant's center frequency. The center frequency is the preferred frequency (resonance frequency) of the associated vocal tract cavity. Components that occur close to the center frequency will be amplified the most, while components that occur somewhat farther away will be amplified to a lesser extent. The BANDWIDTH of a formant is a measure that indicates how wide the sphere of influence of a formant is (how wide the range is of frequencies that are affected).

Formants as seen in spectrograms

Formants can be seen in narrow-band spectrograms as groups of adjacent harmonics (assuming that the source signal is periodic) that are darker than neighboring harmonics.

In broad-band spectrograms, the frequency resolution is normally not fine enough to show separate harmonics. The advantage of this is that, in a broad-band spectrogram, a formant is shown as a single dark horizontal (sometimes tilted or curved) band. Most of the time formants are easy to spot in broad-band spectrograms, particularly those in the lower frequency ranges. For an example, one should look again at the spectrogram in figure 3.11. Formants are clearly seen in the vertically striated areas that belong to the vowels. The easiest formants to spot are the lowest five, which in this example are all located in the frequency range of 0–4,500 Hz.

The presence of a formant structure in spectrograms is a characteristic feature of vowels and other sonorant speech sounds. The perceived phonetic quality of these sonorants depends to a large degree on the (center) frequency of the formants, in particular on the frequency of the lowest two or three formants.

Like harmonics, formants are numbered from bottom to top. The formant with the lowest center frequency is called the first formant, the one with the next lowest frequency is the second formant, and so on. The term "first formant" is often abbreviated as F_1. Likewise, the other formants are abbreviated as F_2, F_3, and so forth. (One should also note that the fundamental frequency of a speech wave is often abbreviated as F_0.)

For identifying formants, a useful rule of thumb is that the average number of formants is one for each frequency band of 1,000 Hz, with the first formant occurring somewhere around 500 Hz. In female voices, formants may be spaced a little more widely, say one in every 1,200 Hz. Of course, this is only a general trend. In specific cases, formants may occur closer together, as in the vowel [u], where both the first and second formants occur below 1,000 Hz.

Formants as seen in spectra

In order to determine the frequency of a formant more precisely, one will normally need to look at a spectrum of the concerned sound. In figure 3.8, arrowheads point to peaks in a spectrum of the vowel [a] that correspond to the first three formants. Most computer software for acoustic analysis will let the user position a cursor at the place of a peak in the spectrum and present a readout of the frequency value at that place.

Often one will also be able to inspect a smoothed spectrum (also seen in figure 3.8), which shows the general trend of the spectrum without showing peaks for the individual harmonics. A smoothed spectrum often gives a better indication of the frequency of formants than a raw spectrum.

As was explained above, a formant is associated with the resonance frequency of a cavity in the vocal tract. Harmonics may occur close to this resonance frequency, but often not exactly *at* the resonance frequency. In this way, within a group of harmonics that are affected by a formant, the harmonic with the greatest intensity may still be, say, 50 Hz or 75 Hz away from the actual resonance frequency. (When formants occur close together, a smoothed spectrum may show a single plateau rather than two separate peaks. In such cases, one needs to look at the raw spectrum as well in order to estimate the location of formants.)

3.2.6 Anti-formants

Whereas formants are regions in a spectrum where frequencies are strengthened, anti-formants (also called anti-resonances or zeros) are regions where frequencies are weakened.

Anti-formants are mostly associated with nasals and nasalized vowels. The lowering of the velum opens an alternative passageway (namely the nose) for the air to flow out. In the case of nasal consonants, there is a complete closure somewhere in the mouth, causing all the air to take the nasal passage. Due to the fact that there is an open connection between the air stream and the oral cavity that it is passing by, the oral cavity absorbs energy in the vicinity of its resonance frequency. In spectrograms, the reduction of energy near a certain frequency shows up as a white (or relatively light) band. In a spectrum, this is seen as a deep valley. An example is given in figure 3.13. In the spectrogram in the upper panel, an ellipse is drawn around the white band associated with an anti-formant in the nasal [m]. In the spectrum in the lower panel, an arrowhead points to the valley that is associated with this same anti-formant.

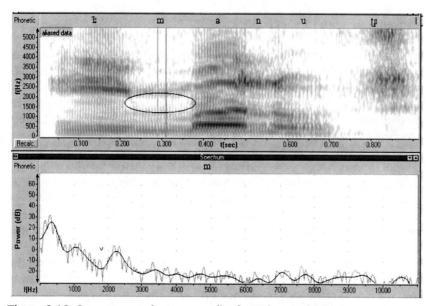

Figure 3.13. Spectrogram (upper panel) of a Kalam Kohistani utterance with ellipse drawn around a low-energy region in the nasal [m] that is associated with an anti-formant; an arrow head points to the corresponding dip in the spectrum (lower panel).

Anti-formants are not always easy to spot. They may occur in the vicinity of a formant, and in such a case, the anti-formant is manifested as a lowering of the intensity of the formant rather than as a spectral valley.

In the case of nasalized vowels, most of the air stream flows out through the mouth. Due to the open connection with the nasal cavity, energy at certain frequencies is absorbed in the nasal cavity, leading to dips or reduced formants in the spectrum of a nasalized vowel.

3.3 Acoustic features of some speech sounds

In the previous section we have learned to recognize a number of important features of speech sounds that can be seen in spectrograms. These are summarized here one more time for the sake of convenience.

An *overall gap* in the spectrogram (no energy seen—or only background noise—from the lowest to the highest frequencies) is associated with a period of silence in the speech signal.

Random waves and short bursts, as produced by friction or plosion (see section 2.2), show up in spectrograms as *continuous energy*, smeared out over the entire frequency range.

Periodicity (speech waves that show a repetitive pattern) is associated with voicing, that is, with the vibration of the vocal folds. It is often recognized in broad-band spectrograms by the presence of vertical striations. These vertical stripes are due to the energy pulses caused by the successive closures of the vocal folds.

Periodic speech waves consist of distinct frequency components (called *harmonics*) that occur at fixed intervals in the frequency range. These harmonics are seen as (more or less) horizontal lines in a narrow-band spectrogram.

Speech sounds are generated by a source (such as the vibrating vocal folds), then travel through a number of cavities in the throat and the mouth, before they finally leave the mouth. The body of air in each cavity has its own resonance frequency. As the air passes through such a cavity, frequency components that are close to that resonance frequency are strengthened. A set of adjacent frequency components that are strengthened (amplified) in this way is called a *formant*. Formants are seen in broad-band spectrograms as dark, horizontal or sometimes tilted bands.

As the air passes by certain side-chambers (such as the nasal cavity when the velum is open), these side-chambers may absorb energy at certain frequencies. A set of adjacent frequency components that are weakened (attenuated) in this way is called an *anti-formant*. Anti-formants are sometimes seen in broad-band spectrograms as relatively light bands.

In the following subsections we will study a number of major classes of speech sounds (vowels, plosives, fricatives) and see how they are characterized in terms of the spectrographic properties listed above. The skills and insights that are gained as we go along will provide a useful foundation for the reader's own application of spectral analysis to phonetic problems.

3.3.1 Vowels

The most important acoustic features of regular, voiced vowels are the frequencies of their formants, in particular of their first two or three formants.

Measuring formant frequencies

In order to determine the formant frequencies of a particular vowel in a recorded utterance, one will normally first look at a spectrogram to find a good place for taking a spectrum. In the spectrum, one then finds the peaks that correspond to the formants and determines the frequencies at which these peaks occur. The section of the vowel over which the spectrum is calculated should be wide enough to include at least one cycle period. In most cases, a width of approximately 20 ms will be a good choice.

Formant measurements of a vowel should be taken somewhere in the middle of the vowel, where its sound is maximally stationary and minimally colored by a preceding or following sound. A steady-state portion of a vowel is seen in a spectrogram as a section with level, rather than rising or falling formants. However, in many cases, especially if the duration of the vowel is short, there is no such steady state. In such cases, one needs to resort to other criteria for determining a good place to measure formants.

One such criterion is to look for a point where the first or second formant (or both) reaches an extreme value. For instance, if a formant rises during the earlier part of a vowel and falls during the later part of the vowel, then the point where the formant reaches its maximum frequency is where one should measure. Likewise, if a formant first falls and then rises again, one should measure at the point where a minimum frequency is reached. These extreme points occur at the moment when the articulators have reached (or have most closely approached) their target positions for the vowel in question.

If there are no such extreme points (formants are only rising or only falling), then another criterion is to look for a portion of the vowel with maximum overall amplitude and take the measurements there. Maximum amplitude will often correspond to a maximally open mouth. Maximum mouth opening in turn is associated with the time of hitting (or approximating) the target configuration for a vowel.

If none of these criteria work, then one should measure formant frequencies at the temporal midpoint of the vowel. (See section 2.4, for some guidelines for determining the boundaries of vowels and consonants.)

Interpreting formant data

In a classical study of the production and perception of American English vowels, Peterson and Barney (1952) presented the following average frequencies for the first three formants of vowels as produced by seventy-six speakers (thirty-three men, twenty-eight women, and fifteen children). Ten different vowels were spoken in the context *h__d* (*heed, hid, head, had, hod, hawed, hood, who'd, hud, heard*). Each vowel was recorded twice for each speaker, giving a total of 76 (speakers) x 10 (vowels) x 2 (repetitions) = 1,520 recorded words. The average formant frequencies for each vowel, as determined by Peterson and Barney, are given in table 3.1.

Table 3.1. Average formant frequencies of American English vowels*

		i	ɪ	ɛ	æ	ɑ	ɔ	ʊ	u	ʌ	ə
F_1	M	270	390	530	660	730	570	440	300	640	490
	W	310	430	610	860	850	590	470	370	760	500
	Ch	370	530	690	1010	1030	680	560	430	850	560
F_2	M	2290	1990	1840	1720	1090	840	1020	870	1190	1350
	W	2790	2480	2330	2050	1220	920	1160	950	1400	1640
	Ch	3200	2730	2610	2320	1370	1060	1410	1170	1590	1820
F_3	M	3010	2550	2480	2410	2440	2410	2240	2240	2390	1690
	W	3310	3070	2990	2850	2810	2710	2680	2670	2780	1960
	Ch	3730	3600	3570	3320	3170	3180	3310	3260	3360	2160

*from Peterson and Barney (1952); M = men, W = women, Ch = children

What we see first of all are the differences between men, women, and children. Average formant frequencies for female speakers are 10–20 percent above those of male speakers, and formant frequencies for children are higher yet. These differences are due to the fact that on average men are bigger than women, and adults are bigger than children. Consequently, the average female vocal tract is shorter than the average male vocal tract, and so the resonance cavities for women are smaller than those for men. Smaller cavities have higher resonance frequencies.

A point to note, then, is that there is a considerable range within which the frequency of a certain formant of a certain vowel may vary. One factor that conditions this variation is vocal tract length: a shorter vocal tract produces higher formant frequencies.

In figure 3.14 we have diagrammed the vowels produced by the adult male speakers, using the average frequencies of the first two formants. In the figure, F_1 has been plotted along the vertical axis, with frequency decreasing as one moves upward in the graph. F_2 has been plotted along the horizontal axis, with frequency once more decreasing as one moves from left to right in the graph.

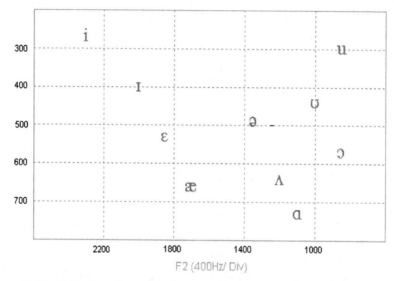

Figure 3.14. F_2-F_1 plot of average formant frequencies of American English vowels as produced by male speakers; from Peterson and Barney (1952).

When we plot vowels in this manner, they are arranged in a way that re-sembles a traditional vowel diagram describing vowels in terms of height and place. In a traditional vowel diagram, the horizontal dimension represents place of articulation (front-back), while the vertical dimension represents tongue height or degree of mouth opening (low-high, open-close).

Apparently there is a correlation between F_1 and vowel height: a high F_1 is associated with a low (open) vowel, and a low F_1 is associated with a high (close) vowel. Also, a high F_2 is associated with a front vowel, while a low F_2 is associated with a back vowel. (Ladefoged and Maddieson, 1996:285, point out, though, that F_1 and F_2 do not reflect only height and place: "In fact, many articulatory adjustments contribute to the values of these acoustic parameters, one of the most important being the effect of lip rounding.")

There are several different ways of plotting formants, that may each pro-vide a somewhat different look at the acoustic vowel space of a language. An important alternative to the example in figure 3.14 is to plot F_1 against the difference of F_2 and F_1, rather than against F_2 directly. Here, F_1 is again plotted from top to bottom, while F_2-F_1 is plotted from right to left.

Another variation is to use a different scale for displaying frequencies. In the example of figure 3.14, simple linear scales are used in the two dimensions. In a linear scale, the same distance represents the same frequency difference in hertz anywhere along the scale. If a distance of 1 cm corresponds to a frequency difference of 200 Hz near the beginning of the scale, then the same will be true further up the scale. However, people do not perceive frequency differences in a linear fashion. A frequency difference of, say, 200 Hz is much more noticeable for people (and perceived as a much greater difference) if lower frequencies are involved (as in the difference between 200 and 400 Hz) than if higher frequencies are involved (as in the difference between 2000 and 2200 Hz). In formant plots of the type shown in figure 3.14, often a scale is used that reflects the way in which people perceive frequency differences. A prominent example of such a perception-based scale is the bark scale (see Traunmüller 1990 for a discussion of such scales).

Spurious formants

The task of determining formant frequencies is sometimes made more difficult when there are peaks in a spectrum that are not due to the usual formants. An example of this is seen in figure 3.15. The figure presents a spectrum of a vowel [i] as spoken by an adult male speaker of Kalam Kohistani. There are decent formant peaks at approximately 260 Hz and 2,300 Hz. These are normal values for the first two formants of a front close vowel. In between these two peaks, however, a much lower peak is seen (indicated by an arrowhead in the figure).

How can the occurrence of such additional peaks be explained? Stevens (1997:474ff.) says that an acoustic model of vowels in terms of a periodic source sound produced at the glottis and resonance cavities that amplify some of the frequencies in the source signal, is only an approximation. It "accounts for the principal attributes of vowel spectra under most conditions." Several situations exist in which this simple model needs modification. One such situation occurs when the velum is lowered, as for nasals and nasalized sounds. Due to the open connection between the oral and nasal cavities there is not only amplification, but also attenuation (weakening) of some frequencies in that case (see section 3.2.6).

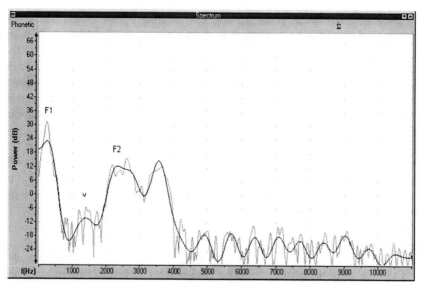

Figure 3.15. Spectrum of the vowel [i] showing an additional peak
(indicated by arrow head) in between F1 and F2.

Another such situation may occur if the opening at the glottis is large
enough for resonances in the windpipe (trachea) to influence the speech
signal. The effect of such an acoustic connection between the vocal tract
and the windpipe is the introduction of additional peaks and valleys in the
spectrum. For adult speakers, the first three of these additional peaks and
valleys occur in the frequency ranges of 600–800 Hz, 1,400–1,800 Hz, and
2,000–2,500 Hz. The one in the range 1,400–1,800 Hz is evident most consistently, according to Stevens. In some speakers these tracheal resonances
are seen more clearly than in other speakers.

The extra peak in figure 3.15, immediately preceded by a sharp valley, may very well be due to such a tracheal resonance. One should also
consider whether the additional peak and valley could be due to a nasal
formant or anti-formant. This is less likely in the given example, which
involves a phonemically oral vowel surrounded by non-nasal sounds. It is
possible, though, that the speaker's velum was not fully closed, perhaps
in anticipation of the [m] occurring in the following word.

3.3.2 Fricatives and plosives

Fricatives

Figures 3.16, 3.17, and 3.18 present spectrograms and spectra of the voiceless fricatives [f], [s], and [x], respectively. All three were spoken by the author, preceded and followed by the vowel [a]. The frequency range displayed in the spectrograms is 0–11,000 Hz.

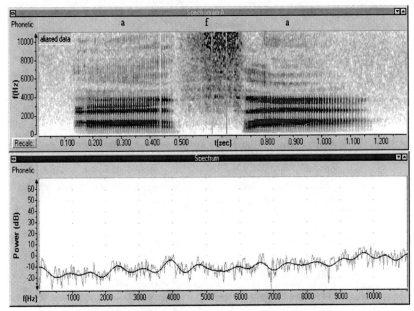

Figure 3.16. Spectrogram of [afa] (upper panel) with spectrum taken in the voiceless labiodental fricative [f].

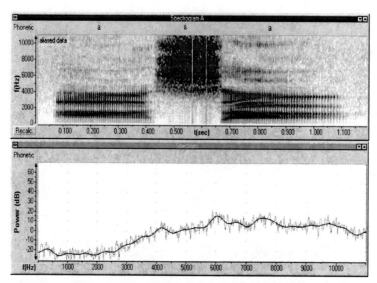

Figure 3.17. Spectrogram of [asa] (upper panel) with spectrum taken in the voiceless alveolar grooved fricative [s].

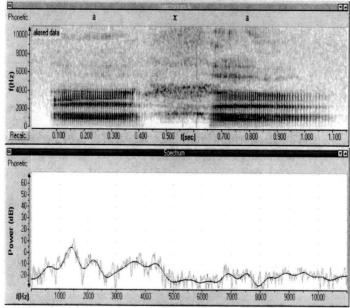

Figure 3.18. Spectrogram of [axa] (upper panel) with spectrum taken in the voiceless velar fricative [x].

The fricatives show up in the spectrograms as clouds of continuous energy. Differences in place of articulation are reflected in the different ways energy is distributed in the frequency dimension. The overall trend of energy distribution can be even, rising or falling as we move from lower to higher frequencies. Also, different fricatives may have energy peaks at different points in the frequency dimension.

The voiceless labiodental fricative [f] (figure 3.16) has energy rather evenly distributed over the spectrum. There are peaks and valleys in the spectrum, but these are not very pronounced.

The voiceless alveolar grooved fricative [s] (figure 3.17) has little energy below 3,000 Hz. The region between 3,000 Hz and 4,000 Hz is characterized by increasing energy. Peaks in the spectrum are seen at approximately 4,200 Hz, 6,100 Hz, and 7,500 Hz.

Whereas the [s] is characterized by a concentration of energy in the higher frequency ranges, the voiceless velar fricative [x] (figure 3.18) shows a concentration of energy in the lower parts of the spectrum. Most of the energy is concentrated below 4,500 Hz. A peak is seen at around 1,500 Hz.

One should be aware that there may be a rather wide range of allophonic variation in the fricatives (and in the plosives). For instance, in front of the vowel [u] the [s] is likely to be pronounced with lip rounding, whereas in front of the vowel [i] it is likely to be pronounced with spread lips. Lip rounding emphasizes lower frequencies as compared to a pronunciation with spread lips. The reader can hear this for her- or himself by conducting the following experiment: produce the fricative [s] and alternatingly round and spread the lips. One will hear an alternation of lower- and higher-pitched hisses.

Another factor is that the place of articulation may vary quite a bit. The [x] in front of [i] is likely to be pronounced much more forward than a [x] in front of [u]. An articulation that is more forward along the roof of the mouth will emphasize higher frequencies as compared to a more backward articulation, even if the lips are held in a constant position. This point, too, can be demonstrated with an experiment: produce a voiceless fricative somewhere in the mouth and slide the tongue forward and backward in the mouth while continuing to produce frication noise. One will hear higher hisses for the more forward tongue positions, and lower hisses for the more backward tongue positions.

Differences between the fricatives can also be seen in the way the formants of the preceding and following vowels transition into and away from the fricative. This phenomenon also occurs with plosives and is discussed in more detail in the immediately following subsection.

Plosives

In the case of plosives, there are two features that provide cues to place of articulation. Firstly, one can take a look at a spectrum of the noise burst of a plosive. The acoustic properties of the burst of a plosive (seen as a spike of energy in a spectrogram) can be studied in the same way as the properties of fricatives. One main difference, of course, is that the duration of a burst is very short.

Another cue to the place of articulation of a plosive is the direction of formant transitions in a following (or preceding) vowel. The three spectrograms in figure 3.19 represent the plosives [p], [t], and [k] spoken in the context [a_a]. When we look at the middle section of the second vowel in all three spectrograms, we see three steady formants at approximately 800 Hz, 1,300 Hz, and 2,200 Hz. When we trace backward in time through the steady-state formants, a point will be reached where these formants start to curve. The formant curves are due to the transition between the vowel and the preceding plosive. It is clearly seen in the figure that the different plosives give rise to different types of bends in the formant trajectories.

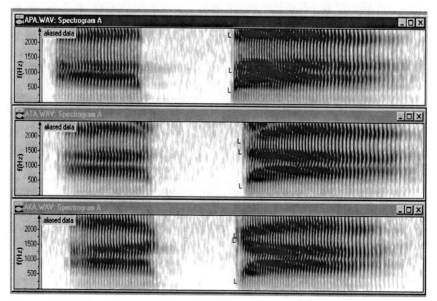

Figure 3.19. Spectrograms of [apa] (upper panel), [ata] (middle panel), and [aka]; L = locus.

When we trace a formant from its steady state in the middle of the vowel backward in the direction of the preceding plosive, and follow the curve that marks the transition between the two sounds, and continue in that direction even after the formant is no longer visible, we will reach the release spike belonging to the plosive. The point at the intersection of the extrapolated formant curve and the start of the release spike is called a LOCUS. A locus is the place from where a formant transition appears to originate. In figure 3.19 we see the lowest three formants of each vowel; the locus of each formant is roughly indicated in the figure by the position of a letter 'L'.

As is seen in the figure, the locus of the first formant (the F_1-locus) is always very low. This is not surprising, as we have already seen in section 3.3.1 that a low F_1 correlates with a high position of the tongue and a relatively closed mouth. More information regarding the place of articulation of a plosive is borne by the F_2-locus. The F_2-locus of a bilabial is relatively low; the F_2-locus of an alveolar is higher, and the F_2-locus of a velar is higher still. In particular, the F_2-locus of a velar plosive is subject to variation, depending on the quality of the vowel. A velar plosive, however, may also be recognized by a converging pattern of F_2 and F_3, resulting in loci which are very close to one another (as seen in figure 3.19).

Preceding vowels carry information about a following plosive in much the same way: one should look at the right-hand part of the vowel, particularly at the area that reflects the transition into the following plosive. The bends in the formants that are seen there are to a large degree a mirror image of the formant transitions seen in the initial part of the following vowel (if the preceding and following vowel are the same, as is the case in the examples).

In figure 3.20, the F_2-locus of the plosive [t] in the context of three different vowels is roughly indicated by the position of the letter 'L'. Whereas the steady-state F_2 of the vowel [i] is very high (around 2,200 Hz), of the vowel [a] very low (around 800 Hz), and of the vowel [u] somewhere in between (around 1,300 Hz), in all three cases the F_2-locus is seen in the region of 1,500–1,900 Hz.

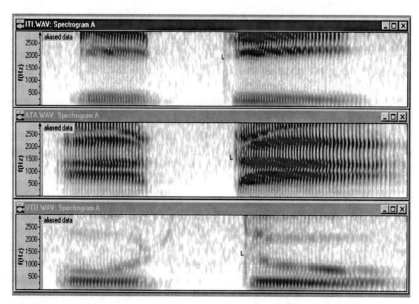

Figure 3.20. Spectrograms of [iti] (upper panel), [ata] (middle panel), and [utu]; L = F₂-locus.

What we have seen is that formant transitions at the beginning (or the end) of a vowel give information about the articulation place of a preceding (or following) plosive. Locus is a useful concept for describing such formant transitions: the steady-state formant frequency defines one end of the transition, the locus frequency defines the other end. We should remind ourselves, though, that a locus is not something that can be seen in a spectrogram. It is determined by tracing and extrapolating a curving formant into the spike.

3.3.3 Static versus dynamic features

In concluding this chapter, a word is in order about the distinction between static and dynamic spectral characteristics of speech sounds. When we looked at the acoustic properties of vowels, and especially at the role that formants play in defining the characteristic quality of a vowel, we were looking at STATIC properties (the notion of change did not play a role in the discussions).

However, in the previous subsection we looked at formant transitions that provide information about the articulation place of a neighboring sound. At that point we were looking at DYNAMIC aspects of spectrograms (namely formant frequencies that were changing over time).

In the acoustic study of speech sounds, it is important not to overlook such dynamic characteristics. For instance, in the case of nasal consonants, information about articulation place is borne by formant transitions between a nasal and a neighboring vowel in much the same way as in the case of plosives. For an example, one should look once more at the upper panel in figure 3.13 (repeated here as figure 3.21), in particular at the second formant of the vowel [a] seen in the middle of the spectrogram. Tracing this formant backwards from right to left, we see a falling curve which levels off at a frequency of around 1,000 Hz once we reach the preceding nasal [m]. This transition is rather similar to the one that occurs before the plosive [p] in the upper panel of figure 3.19.

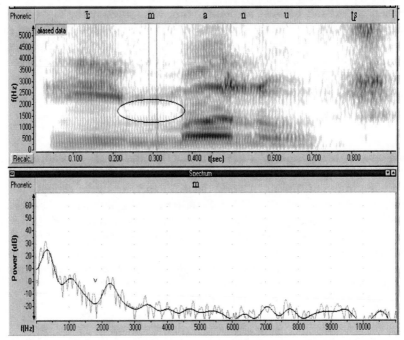

Figure 3.21 Spectrogram (upper panel) of a Kalam Kohistani utterance (repeated from Figure 3-13)

If we look once more at the F_2 transition in figure 3.21 and trace it from left to right into the following nasal [n], we see that it levels off at approximately 1,500 Hz. This is similar to the F_2-locus seen for the plosive [t] in figure 3.19. Again, we see that formant changes during the production of a vowel are important, as they provide information about the identity of a neighboring sound.

An instructive experiment in this regard is the following: record a syllable consisting of a plosive followed by a vowel. In a waveform editor, place the cursor at the boundary of the plosive and the vowel; all of the noise burst of the plosive should be included on the left side of the cursor. Now if one listens selectively to the wave on the left side of the cursor, one will hear the plosive. If one listens selectively to the wave on the right side of the cursor, one will hear the vowel. If the experiment is successful, then one will be able to say from listening to the vowel only, what the articulation place of the preceding plosive is.

As a final example of the importance of dynamic features, we may consider diphthongs. The acoustic properties of a diphthong cannot be measured at a single point in time, because no point in time can represent the diphthong as a whole. The essence of a diphthong is changing vowel quality, reflected in a spectrogram as gliding formant trajectories. A simple approach to diphthongs is to describe them in terms of a transition from an initial state (character-ized by a set of frequencies for F_1, F_2, and possibly F_3) to a final state (also characterized by a set of formant frequencies).

3.4 Further reading

This chapter provides only a first introduction to the art of reading spec-trograms and spectra. There is no space to discuss the acoustic properties of a wide range of sounds. A good place for further study, though, is the book by Peter Ladefoged and Ian Maddieson: *The Sounds of the World's Languages* (1996, Oxford: Blackwell Publishers), a book that is indispensable for any linguistic field library. Similarly indispensable are two other books by Peter Ladefoged: *Vowels and Consonants: An Introduction to the Sounds of Languages* (2000) and *Phonetic Data Analysis: An Introduction to Fieldwork and Instrumental Techniques* (2003).

4

Voice and Aspiration

In speech, three mechanisms are used for generating sound: plosion, frication, and voice. In order to produce PLOSION, an air pressure difference is built up between the two sides of a closure in the vocal tract. The release of this closure causes a sudden stream of air that sets off sound vibrations. In the case of FRICATION, turbulences are generated by forcing air through a narrow constriction somewhere in the vocal tract. (Additional turbulences are generated when an airstream breaks against an obstacle in its way, such as the teeth.) Third, there is VOICED SOUND, which is produced by a repetitive closing and opening of the vocal folds while air is flowing out from the lungs.

The sound signals that are produced at these sources are modified as they travel through a number of resonance cavities in the vocal tract and pass by side chambers. The resonance cavities will strengthen certain frequencies or frequency bands in the sound signal; the side chambers may absorb energy and thereby weaken certain frequencies in the signal. In this way, the resonances and anti-resonances add a specific coloring to the source sound, resulting in audible differences between for instance [e] and [o], or between [s] and [ʃ].

All languages have sounds that are voiced (the sound source is the vibration of the vocal folds; note that this source may be combined with a second source, as in the case of voiced plosives and voiced fricatives) and sounds that are voiceless (the sound source is frication or plosion; there is no vocal fold vibration). Many languages use the difference between voiced and voiceless sounds contrastively, that is: to mark the difference between pairs of phonemes, distinguishing for example [t] from [d] or [s] from [z]. In many languages the difference also plays a role subphonemically, when a certain phoneme has voiced and voiceless allophones.

When there is vocal fold vibration (phonation), it may be of different types. In the phonetic literature a range of modes of phonation is distinguished. There is a continuum of possibilities that is associated with the closeness of the vocal folds: held farther apart or held closer together (Ladefoged and Maddieson 1996:49). For the purpose of this chapter we will divide the continuum into three categories only: BREATHY VOICE (vocal folds held farther apart; they vibrate, but the closures are not complete; air leaks through the glottis even during the closures; there is a relatively high rate of airflow), MODAL VOICE (normal, regular voice; the folds are held close together, allowing for regular vibration with full periodic closures of the glottis), and CREAKY

VOICE (vocal folds held strongly together; airflow through the glottis is less than in modal voice; vibration is slow and irregular).

When the vocal folds are held wide apart, air can flow through the glottis without causing the folds to vibrate. Normally no sound will be generated at the glottis under this condition. However, a high speed of airflow through the open glottis will cause turbulences around the glottis, even if the folds are wide open (as in panting or wheezing). This is in fact frication produced at or near the glottis. The voiceless glottal fricative [h] is produced in this way. ASPIRATION is glottal frication immediately following (sometimes preceding) a closure or narrow constriction in the vocal tract.

In this chapter we will look at some acoustic features of voicing. In section 4.1 we will discuss differences between the three modes of phonation mentioned above. In section 4.2 we will look more closely at the distinction of phonemically voiced versus voiceless consonants and how it may be reflected in the acoustic properties of the sound signal. In that section we will also look at the distinction between voiceless aspirated and unaspirated consonants.

4.1 Studying phonation types

In this section we distinguish three modes of phonation: modal voice, breathy voice, and creaky voice. These different modes of phonation produce different sound qualities. When our interest is in features that may be distinctive for the phonemes of a language, we usually speak of types of voicing, or types of phonation. When our interest is in larger stretches of speech, or even in the characteristics of a certain speaker, we more usually speak of voice quality or voice register.

Modal voice, breathy voice, and creaky voice may function at the phonemic (and subphonemic) level in a language, but they may also characterize larger stretches of speech. There are other types of phonation that may characterize larger stretches of speech, but are not used at the (sub-) phonemic level in languages. Examples of that are HARSH VOICE (involving very strong tension of the vocal folds) and FALSETTO (vocal folds stretched lengthwise; high rate of vibration involving only a part of the length of the folds).

4.1.1 Inverse filtering

Unfortunately, it is practically impossible to record and analyze directly the sound generated by the vibrating vocal folds. The sound that we hear and can record through a microphone is always distorted by the resonances and antiresonances in the vocal tract. To get rid of any vocal tract effects on the source sound signal, we would have to lay bare the vocal folds by removing the speaker's head, and hope that he or she will nevertheless continue speaking in that unpleasant condition! In view of this difficulty, techniques have been developed for studying the characteristics of the source sound indirectly. One of these is called INVERSE FILTERING. We will briefly discuss this technique here, but will conclude that it is not practical for fieldworkers. (The reader can skip to section 4.1.2 without missing information that is essential to the understanding of the rest of the chapter.)

In inverse filtering one records speech sound as it flows out from the mouth and then applies mathematical procedures to undo the effects of the resonances and anti-resonances in the vocal tract. The vocal tract is thought of as a filter that selectively strengthens certain frequencies in the source signal and weakens others (see section 3.2.5). When we record a sound at the lips, and want to reconstruct the source sound as it was at the glottis, then we can pass the output sound through a filter that does exactly the opposite of what the vocal tract filter did. Frequencies that were amplified in the vocal tract should be attenuated; frequencies that were attenuated should be amplified. This, of course, requires that we have a good model of the vocal tract filter to begin with.

While the idea of inverse filtering is not difficult, its execution is. The following passages are taken from Ní Chasaide and Gobl (1997:431f.):

> Inverse filtering based on the speech pressure waveform can yield detailed temporal and spectral information. However, the recording equipment and room are critical, and shortcomings in either condition can lead to disappointing results (...). Ideally, an anechoic chamber should be used. The recording equipment must preserve the phase characteristics of the signal even at very low frequencies, which effectively means that a digital or FM recorder is needed unless the recording is done straight to the computer. Analog recorders introduce phase distortion (...).
>
> For a successful source analysis, it is of course essential that the estimate of the vocal tract transfer function [i.e. the effects of the vocal tract filter] be accurate. (...) At present the most accurate source signal is obtained by using a method where the user interactively fine-tunes the formant frequencies and bandwidths of the inverse filter.
>
> [T]he manual interactive method is not suited to the analysis of large amounts of data. As the analysis typically proceeds on a pulse-by-pulse basis, it is extremely time-consuming.

The technique of inverse filtering, then, is still confined to the phonetics laboratory. It requires an experienced researcher and takes a lot of time.

4.1.2 Studying the output speech signal

Given the difficulties with direct registration of the voice source, as well as with reconstruction of the voice source through inverse filtering, the field linguist is practically limited to studying acoustic features of the output speech signal itself. As different types of phonation lead to audible differences in sound quality, one would expect these differences to show up in acoustic analysis, too.

While a lot of research still needs to be done in this respect, there are a few findings that may be of help to field linguists. Ladefoged and Maddieson (1996:317) write:

> As a general rule, vowels with stiff voice or creaky voice have more energy in the harmonics in the region of the first and second formants than those with modal voice. Conversely, vowels with slack or breathy voice have comparatively more energy in the fundamental frequency. There is also a tendency (though not in all languages) for vowels with creaky voice to have a more irregular vocal fold pulse rate (more jitter), and for breathy voice vowels to have more random energy (a larger noise component) in the higher frequencies.

Spectral composition

As far as spectral composition (as seen in spectrograms and spectra) is concerned, there are two measures that are frequently used in the literature as indicators of the mode of voiced phonation. For a good use of these measures it is desirable that the speech items that are compared be identical, except for the phonation type difference. In addition, as there may be vast differences between speakers in overall voice quality (some persons may generally tend to speak in a more breathy voice, other persons may tend to speak in a tense or harsh voice, and so on), it is good practice to make comparisons between one and the same speaker.

One indicator, then, is the difference of the intensities of the first and second harmonics. The intensity level of the first harmonic is often abbreviated as H_1, while that of the second harmonic is abbreviated as H_2, and so the indicator that we are interested in can be written as H_1-H_2 ("H_1 minus H_2"). (See section 3.2.4 for an explanation of harmonics.)

In order to determine H_1-H_2, one first needs to calculate a spectrum over an appropriate section of the concerned speech sound. The section of the sound over which the spectrum is calculated should be wide enough to include at least one cycle period. In most cases, a width of approximately 20 ms will be a good choice. (See sections 3.1.4 and 3.3.1 for more information on spectra.)

In the raw spectrum (a smoothed spectrum does not show the individual harmonics), one finds the first harmonic and reads off its intensity level (this is usually expressed in decibels, abbreviated as dB), which gives us H_1. Next, one finds the second harmonic and determines H_2.

(As a check on the correct identification of the first harmonic, one can compare its frequency readout with the fundamental frequency of the speech wave at that point in the utterance, as given in an F_0 graph. These should be roughly the same—in theory they should be exactly the same, but due to limitations of acoustic speech analysis procedures one may get somewhat different values. The frequency of the second harmonic should roughly be twice the fundamental frequency. (See section 5.2.1 for more information on extracting the fundamental frequency.)

The value of H_1-H_2 should be compared between the members of a minimal pair or minimal set. A relatively large positive difference (showing a strong H_1) is indicative of breathy voice. In modal voice the difference will be smaller, or H_2 may even be stronger than H_1. In creaky voice, H_2 may be stronger still. Of course, if the second harmonic is located in the neighborhood of the first formant, then that may boost the value of H_2, affecting the value of H_1-H_2 as well.

An example from the Torwali language of Pakistan is presented in figure 4.1. The example involves a contrast between a regularly voiced vowel [o] and one that is partially breathy-voiced: [o̤o]. The spectra were calculated over 25 ms sections starting at the beginning of each vowel. In the second item, breathy voice occurred during the initial 80 ms of the vowel. (The breathy-voiced part of this vowel might be analysed as belonging to the preceding plosive, and that plosive could then be called a "breathy-voiced" or "voiced aspirated" plosive. If the breathy-voiced portion is assigned to the vowel, we would transcribe the word as [go̤o] If it is assigned to the plosive, it would be [gʱo]. Both are possible interpretations of the same phonetic facts. Which one makes more sense for Torwali is yet to be determined.)

It can be seen in the examples that both vowels have a low first formant at around 300 Hz. The second and third harmonics are nearest to this formant, and so in our comparison of the intensity levels of the first and second harmonics we must consider that the level of the second harmonic has been boosted by the first formant. Even so, the first harmonic is very strong in the breathy-voiced example (lower panel in figure 4.1), stronger than the second harmonic. On the other hand, H_2 is greater than H_1 in the example with modal voice (upper panel).

An alternative measure takes H_1 and compares it, not with H_2, but with the intensity level of the first formant. The latter is often abbreviated as A_1

(A for 'amplitude'). A relatively strong H_1 is again indicative of breathy voice. A relatively strong A_1 may indicate creaky voice.

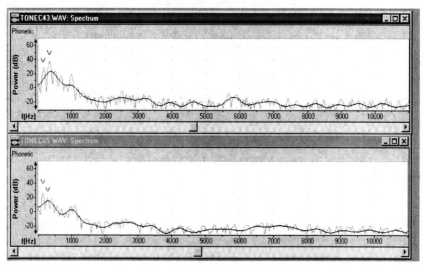

Figure 4.1. Spectra of regular voiced vowel [o] (upper panel) and breathy-voiced vowel[o̤] taken from Torwali [go] 'ox' and [go̤o̤] 'horse': arrowheads point to the first and second harmonics.

This is illustrated by a finding by Ladefoged and Maddieson (1996:317ff.), who present data for Jalapa Mazatec, a language that has a three-way vowel contrast of modal voice versus creaky voice versus breathy voice. They recorded a near-minimal set (three items) as produced by five different speakers and determined H_1-A_1 for each item and each speaker. Considerable variation was found between speakers, but for all speakers the average value of H_1-A_1 was higher for breathy voice than for modal voice, while in turn the average value for modal voice was higher than for creaky voice.

Another example from Torwali is presented in figure 4.2, involving the items [bal] 'hair' (modal voice, upper panel) and [ba̤a̤] 'brother' (breathy voice). This time the left arrowhead points to the first harmonic, and the right arrowhead points to the harmonic that is closest to the frequency of the first formant. In the example, the latter happens to be the third harmonic. The examples show a relatively strong H_1 in the breathy-voiced item as opposed to a stronger A_1 in the modally-voiced item.

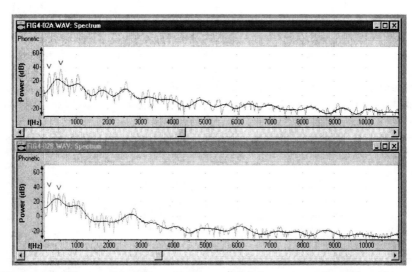

Figure 4.2. Spectra of regular voiced vowel [a] (upper panel) and breathy-voiced vowel [a̤], taken from Torwali [bal] 'hair' and [ba̤a̤] 'brother'; the leftmost arrowheads point to the first *harmonic,* while those to the right point to the harmonic that is closest to the first *formant.*

Due to the fact that air leaks through the vocal folds during breathy voice, even at the moments when the glottis is maximally closed, some glottal frication is produced. Therefore, another indication of breathy voice may be the presence of a relatively large amount of noise (Ladefoged and Maddieson 1996:317). This is seen in a spectrogram as a relatively dark cloud. (A clear example of this is shown in Ladefoged and Maddieson 1996:59, figure 3.6.)

Some speech analysis packages enable one to calculate the HARMONICS-TO-NOISE RATIO (HNR). The amount of energy contained in the harmonics is divided by the energy of the noise, giving the HNR. If the ratio is high, the noise is relatively weak. If the ratio is low, the noise is relatively strong. The latter may be an indication of breathiness (granted that we are comparing utterances of similar recording quality).

Speech wave graph (speech waveform)

Apart from spectral composition, cues to the type of voiced phonation may also be present in the speech waveform. As was said above, breathy voice may be accompanied by glottal frication, and when this is strong enough it may be seen as random energy in a spectrogram, but also as random, rapid fluctuations superimposed on a periodic wave in a speech wave graph. (For a good example, see Ladefoged and Maddieson 1996:319, figure 9.32.)

Creaky voice is associated with slow and at times irregular vibrations of the vocal folds. Figure 4.3 repeats an example from figure 2.23, showing an utterance in Kalam Kohistani. The vowel [a] of the word [bal] 'hair' is partially creaky-voiced. An enlargement of the creaky-voiced part is shown in the lower panel in the figure.

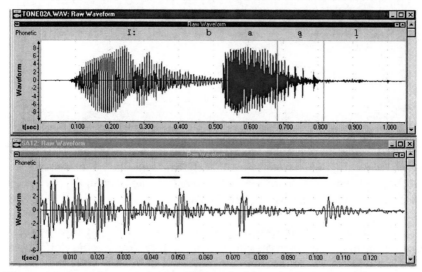

Figure 4.3. Speech wave graph of Kalam Kohistani utterance, with expanded view of creaky-voiced vowel [a] (lower panel); line segments indicate the distance from one glottal pulse to the the next at different positions in the vowel.

The three horizontal line segments drawn above the waveform in the lower panel indicate the distance between two voicing pulses at different points in the vowel. At the place where the second line segment is drawn, the time interval between two pulses is suddenly twice as long as it was during the preceding three periods of the wave (the second line segment is roughly twice as long as the first). The third line segment is even more than three times as long as the first one. Whereas in modal voice the time interval between voicing pulses (which is equal to the cycle period of the wave) is constant, or changes only gradually, in this example of creaky voice we see abrupt, major changes in the length of this interval.

4.2 Voiced, voiceless, and aspirated plosives

4.2.1 Acoustic features correlating with the voiced-voiceless distinction

Dutch is one of many languages that have a contrastive distinction between voiced and voiceless plosives. Figure 4.4 shows an example of [d] and [t] contrasting in identical environments. The terms voiced and voiceless suggest that the primary phonetic distinction between these two consonants is the presence versus absence of vocal fold vibration. However, an acoustic study of the contrast shows that there are other phonetic differences as well, and that vocal fold vibration may actually not be the most consistent cue to voicing.

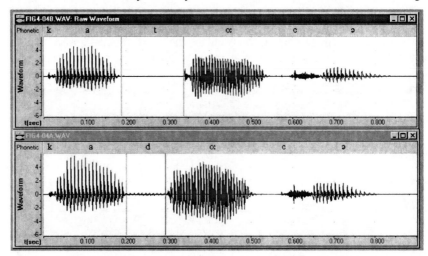

Figure 4.4. Speech wave graphs of Dutch *Katootje* (a girl's name) and *kadootje* 'a present', showing voiceless [t] (upper panel) and voiced [d] in identical environments; vertical lines mark off the closure phase of both consonants.

It is clear in the given example that the closure phase of the voiced plosive (lower panel) is filled with a low-intensity periodic sound signal, which is due to the continuing vibration of the vocal folds. During the closure of the voiceless plosive (upper panel), on the other hand, no signal is seen at all. Indeed, presence versus absence of vocal fold vibration is associated with the voiced-voiceless distinction in this example.

At the same time, another acoustic difference is easily noticed in the figure: the closure phase of the [t] is much longer (151 ms in this example) than that of the [d] (97 ms). In fact, the duration of the voiceless plosive as a whole is quite a bit longer than the duration of the voiced plosive.

It is also true in this example that the vowel preceding the voiceless plosive is shorter (159 ms) than the vowel preceding the voiced plosive (166 ms). These durational patterns have been observed for many languages: voiceless plosives are longer in duration than voiced plosives, while vowels preceding voiceless plosives are shorter than vowels preceding voiced plosives (assuming that we compare identical vowels in environments that are identical—apart from the voicing distinction between the plosives). The duration of the preceding vowel, one can say, tends to compensate for the duration of the plosive.

Turning to figure 4.5, we see another acoustic feature that accompanies the voiced-voiceless distinction. Figure 4.5 presents F_0 (fundamental frequency) graphs for the same items. (Notice that the F_0 curves are interrupted during voiceless consonants due to the absence of vocal fold vibration; there is also an interruption during the [d]: there is vocal fold vibration, as we saw in figure 4.4, but the signal in this example is too weak for the F_0 extraction algorithm and is not registered—see chapter 5 for more information on F_0 extraction procedures.)

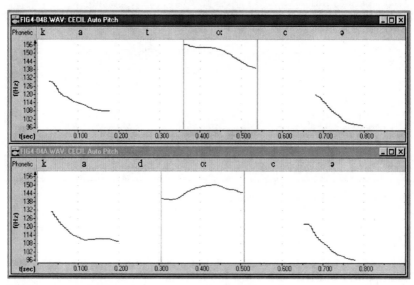

Figure 4.5. Fundamental frequency graphs of Dutch *Katootje* (a girl's name) and *kadootje* 'a present'; vertical lines mark off the vowel following voiceless [t] or voiced [d].

As is illustrated here, F_0 is another cue to look for in identifying voiced-voiceless distinctions. The graphs in the upper and lower panels of figure 4.5 are very similar, except for the part occurring during the vowel [o:]. In the upper panel, the vowel [o:] follows the voiceless [t]; its F_0 starts out high (at

158 Hz) and gradually falls during the vowel. In the lower panel, the vowel follows the voiced [d]; F_0 starts out much lower (at 141 Hz), rises to a maximum near the middle of the vowel and then starts to fall. This pattern has been observed for a wide range of languages: F_0 starts out relatively high on a vowel following a voiceless plosive, and relatively low on a vowel following a voiced plosive.

Yet another phonetic difference between the two plosives is seen in figure 4.6. The figure shows waveforms of the release bursts of the [t] (upper panel) and the [d]. When we look at the positive amplitudes (distance from zero to peaks of the wave) and negative amplitudes (distance from zero to bottoms of the wave), we see that in the case of the burst of the voiceless [t] the fluctuations generally have greater amplitudes as compared to the burst of the voiced [d], especially during the first half of the bursts. We also see that the burst of the [t] is longer in duration, and we can sum both observations up by saying that the burst of the voiceless plosive has more energy than the burst of the voiced plosive. Again, this is an illustration of a tendency that has been observed more widely.

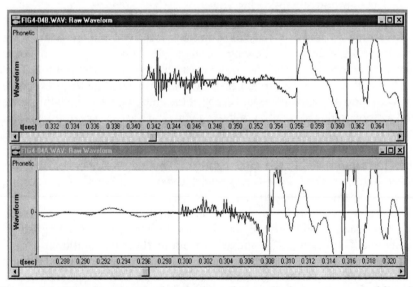

Figure 4.6. Speech wave graphs of release bursts (in between vertical lines) of voiceless [t] (upper panel) and voiced [d].

What we have seen so far is that a voiced plosive may be distinguished from its voiceless counterpart by the following acoustic features:

1. A weak, periodic signal immediately precedes the release burst of the voiced plosive;
2. The duration of the voiced plosive is shorter;
3. The duration of a vowel preceding the voiced plosive is longer;
4. F_0 on a vowel following the voiced plosive starts out lower; and
5. The release burst of the voiced plosive has less energy (smaller amplitude and shorter duration).

It is generally reported that none of these is a necessary acoustic correlate of voiced plosives. Rather, the presence of a subset of these features is sufficient for the perception of voice.

The features discussed so far do not exhaust the ones mentioned in the phonetic literature, although they are the ones that are observed more easily and consistently. Other features include:

6. The abruptness of the transition between the plosive and adjoining vowels; and
7. The duration of a following vowel.

Regarding (6): formant transition durations at the end of a preceding vowel and at the beginning of a following vowel may be longer in the case of voiced plosives and shorter in the case of voiceless plosives (see sections 3.3.2 and 3.3.3 for information on formant transitions). Corresponding features seen in the waveform are: a more gradual decay of the amplitude of a preceding vowel and a more gradual onset of a following vowel in the case of voiced plosives, as opposed to more abrupt amplitude changes in the case of voiceless plosives.

As to (7), a vowel following a voiced plosive may be longer in duration than the same vowel in the same context following a voiceless plosive (this vowel duration effect, however, is reported more consistently for preceding vowels than for following vowels).

For an early, extensive discussion of acoustic correlates of the voiced-voiceless distinction in Dutch, see Slis and Cohen (1969). For English see Lisker and Abramson (1970) and other work by these two authors.

The occurrence of a periodic sound signal during a time interval directly preceding the release burst (sometimes called "voice lead" or "pre-voicing") is a strong cue to the voicedness of a plosive: if it is present, then it is very likely that we are dealing with a voiced rather than a voiceless plosive. However, this is true only from an acoustic point of view. From a perceptual point of view (focussing on the question as to what information is relevant to the listener) the presence or absence of voice lead may be insignificant. For an illustration, look at figure 4.7.

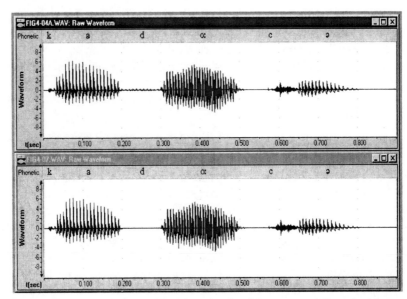

Figure 4.7. Voiced plosive [d] with voice lead (upper panel) and without voice lead.

The speech wave shown in the lower panel of figure 4.7 is the result of a manipulation by means of waveform editing: the word *kadootje* with the voiced [d] was taken (repeated in the upper panel), and the 97 ms of voice lead were replaced by 97 ms of silence. When the two are played back, it appears that no difference whatsoever can be heard between the original and the manipulated utterance.

It should be said that the presence of voice lead may be more noticeable in other items, particularly in items where the plosive occurs utterance initially: if we repeat the experiment with an initial plosive (a plosive that is preceded by a period of silence), then the difference between an original version with voice lead and a manipulated version where voice lead is removed will more often be audible. Even there, though, the phonemic identity of the plosive may not be affected when voice lead is removed: when native speakers listen to the manipulated version (with voice lead removed), they may still recognize the initial plosive as a voiced one rather than a voiceless one.

At any rate, what we see is that the presence of vocal fold vibration is not a necessary phonetic feature of phonologically voiced plosives. Rather there appears to be a *cluster of cues* that conspire to bring about the perception of a plosive as voiced rather than voiceless. If one of these cues is absent, the presence of the other cues is still sufficient for voice perception.

Finally, quite a few of the features discussed here also play a role in the voiced-voiceless distinction for fricatives: presence versus absence of periodicity (associated with vocal fold vibration), shorter duration of voiced fricatives as compared to their voiceless counterparts, longer duration of vowels adjoining voiced fricatives, smaller intensity of the friction noise in the case of voiced fricatives, and lower initial F_0 on vowels following a voiced fricative (see again Slis and Cohen 1969).

4.2.2 Voice onset time (VOT)

The examples of voiced plosives discussed above were taken from Dutch, which is a language where voiced plosives usually have a voice lead. In contrast, English is a language where "voiced" plosives usually do not have a voice lead. In other words, English is a language where phonologically voiced plosives are, strictly speaking, phonetically voiceless (there is no vocal fold vibration during the closure and release of the plosive).

A series of studies by Lisker and Abramson in the 1960s (see for instance their 1970 paper) has shown that it is still possible to view the phonetic distinction between English voiced and voiceless plosives as primarily a voicing distinction. In order to do so, we have to consider the timing of the moment of voice onset (that is: the timing of the start of vocal fold vibration). Lisker and Abramson proposed to take the start of the release of the plosive as a reference time. When we give this reference time a value of zero, then a moment following the release will have a positive time, and a moment preceding the release will have a negative time (-100 ms will mean: '100 ms before the beginning of the release burst'). VOICE ONSET TIME (VOT) is the moment at which the vocal folds start to vibrate, measured in reference to the time of release of the plosive.

Voice onset times can be plotted along a continuous scale, which is normally drawn as a horizontal line with zero in the middle, negative values to the left of zero, and positive values to the right. When we measure VOTs and plot them along such a scale, the similarity between English and Dutch plosives is that voiced plosives are associated with VOTs that occur more to the left on the scale, while the VOTs of voiceless plosives occur more to the right. In other words: in both languages voicing starts earlier in the case of voiced plosives, and later in the case of voiceless plosives. The difference between the two languages is that, overall, the VOTs of Dutch plosives occur more to the left on the scale, while the VOTs of English plosives occur more to the right; in comparison to Dutch plosives, the timing of voice onset in English plosives (both voiced and voiceless) is delayed.

If we use the terms early, medium, and late for VOTs around -80 ms (early), $+10$ ms (medium), and $+80$ ms (late), respectively, then we can say that the timing of voice onset is early for Dutch voiced plosives and medium for Dutch voiceless plosives. On the other hand, the timing of voice onset is medium for English voiced plosives and late for English voiceless plosives.

If the timing of voice onset is late (or greater than, say, +30 ms), then there is an interval between the actual release burst and the start of the following vowel. This interval is normally filled with glottal frication noise, also called aspiration. As this noise is produced at the glottis it will have to travel through the entire vocal tract before it leaves the mouth, and as it does so it will pick up a spectral coloring that resembles the quality of the following vowel (the articulators will be on their way to assume the target configurations for that vowel, or may even have reached them already).

With the VOT scale it is possible to view voice, voicelessness, and aspiration of plosives as categories that occur at different points along one and the same dimension. For a language such as Thai, which has a three-way phonemic contrast of voiced versus voiceless unaspirated versus voiceless aspirated plosives, Lisker and Abramson (1970) showed that differences in VOT are sufficient for the purpose of cueing perception of voice and aspiration. In their experiments on Thai, in which synthetic speech was used, they found that early VOT consistently resulted in the perception of a voiced plosive, medium VOT in the perception of a voiceless unaspirated plosive, and late VOT in the perception of a voiceless aspirated plosive.

What we have seen in this section is that the distinction between two types of plosives that is traditionally described as the presence versus the absence of voicing, is acoustically not always associated with the presence versus the absence of a periodic sound source. Periodicity may be completely absent during a certain plosive, while it may still be perceived as "voiced." A more consistent acoustic correlate of the distinction is voice onset time: "voiced" plosives are associated with an earlier voice onset time, while "voiceless" plosives are associated with a later voice onset time.

In addition there appears to be a range of other features that occur as acoustic correlates of the voiced-voiceless distinction, and these can be perceptually relevant as well.

Voiceless aspiration is a condition which occurs when voice onset time is late; the interval between the release burst and the onset of voicing is filled with glottal frication noise.

5

Prosody

5.1 Introduction

5.1.1 Prosody

In the previous chapters we have been concerned mainly with the properties of vowels and consonants. In this chapter we will look at acoustic aspects of so-called PROSODIC FEATURES. Prosodic features are features that cannot be derived from the intrinsic properties of the vowels and consonants that make up an utterance. They typically stretch out over domains that are wider than a single segment. Examples of prosodic features are stress, tone, and intonation.

The word prosody is derived from Greek *prosôidía* 'song sung to instrumental music' (*ôidê* = 'song, ode', *pros* = 'with'). Early on in Greek, the word came to be used to refer to unwritten features of the pronunciation of words, including pitch and length, and when written marks were introduced to indicate such features, these marks were also called "prosodies." By the second century A.D., the word prosody was already being used to refer quite generally to features of pronunciation that were not expressed in the segmental succession of vowels and consonants (Couper-Kuhlen 1986:1).

Our use of prosody will be more or less synonymous with the term SUPRASEGMENTALS, which used to be more customary among linguists working in the American structuralist tradition. Couper-Kuhlen (1986:2) is careful to point out that the terms prosody and suprasegmentals are not wholly synonymous. Use of one rather than the other carries with it special connotations and often serves to indicate where one's linguistic loyalties are. For a good discussion of these differences, the reader is referred to Couper-Kuhlen (1986).

5.1.2 Phonetic domains of prosody

Strictly speaking, terms such as stress, tone, and intonation refer to linguistic (emic) concepts, not to physical phenomena that can be directly observed and measured. High tones and low tones, final stress and initial stress, rising and falling intonation contours, etc., are elements that play a role in the description of a language system. A language system is something that is intimately known by the speakers of that language, but it is not something that can be directly observed.

Speech, on the other hand, is something that occurs in the observable, physical world: somebody's vocal folds vibrate, a sound wave is propagated through the air, and registered by somebody else's ear. The question to ask, therefore, is: how are the distinctions that are made by a language system reflected in speech? Conversely: what do the observable properties of speech tell us about the system of a language?

Phonetics, the scientific study of speech, is often described as consisting of three domains: ARTICULATORY PHONETICS studies speech from the perspective of the speaker (how is it produced?); AUDITORY PHONETICS studies speech from the perspective of the listener (how is it perceived?); ACOUSTIC PHONETICS studies speech as it travels through the air in the shape of sound waves.

Linguistic distinctions of stress, tone, and intonation are reflected in speech in different configurations of pitch, length, and loudness. The latter three terms actually refer to the domain of auditory phonetics. Pitch, for instance, is a term that refers to an auditory (perceptual) phenomenon. It is associated in the articulatory domain with the rate of vibration of the vocal folds. Both perceived pitch and vocal fold vibration are associated in the acoustic domain with fundamental frequency. The vocal folds vibrate at a certain rate; they produce a sound wave that has a certain fundamental frequency; this wave is registered by a human ear and perceived as a sound with a certain pitch.

In the same way, loudness is associated with the amount of energy (physical effort) expended in articulation, and with intensity in the acoustic domain.

Perceived length correlates with the timing of articulatory movements, and with acoustic duration. This state of affairs is represented in table 5.1 (adapted from Couper-Kuhlen 1986:7):

Table 5.1 Phonetic domains of prosody

Articulatory	Acoustic	Auditory
Rate of vibration of the vocal folds	Fundamental frequency	Pitch
Timing of articulatory movements	Duration	Length
Physical effort	Intensity (amplitude)	Loudness

It is good to note that relations between parameters occurring on the same row in the chart are not entirely simple. It is roughly true, to give an example, that an increase of the rate of vibration of the vocal folds leads to an increased fundamental frequency and to a higher perceived pitch. However, there are a number of distorting factors that we have to take into account. First, there is a perceptual threshold for fundamental frequency differences, such that differences smaller than the threshold are not noticeable to the human ear. Small changes in fundamental frequency may thus not always result in changes in perceived pitch.

Second, we have to take into account that scaling may be different in the different domains. A fundamental frequency difference of, say, 30 Hz is perceived as a large pitch difference if the frequencies involved are low (such as the difference between 90 and 120 Hz), and as a small pitch difference if the frequencies involved are much higher (such as the difference between 360 and 390 Hz).

Third, there may be interactions with other parameters. For instance, an increase in intensity may have an effect on the perception of pitch (resulting e.g. in higher perceived pitch).

In the remainder of this chapter, we will first look in more detail at the acoustic parameters of prosody, which are: fundamental frequency, duration, and intensity. Following that, we will discuss the linguistic features of stress, tone, and intonation, and how they may be studied from an acoustic point of view.

5.2 Fundamental frequency (F$_0$)

A periodic speech wave consists of a sequence of more-or-less similar oscillation patterns (wave cycles). The rate at which these wave cycles are repeated is called the FUNDAMENTAL FREQUENCY of the speech wave, which is abbreviated as F$_0$. Fundamental frequency can be expressed in cycles per second, for which hertz is commonly used as a language-independent term (abbreviated Hz).

Periodic speech waves are generated by means of vocal fold vibration (the repetitive opening and closing of the vocal folds), and the fundamental frequency of speech waves is associated with the rate of vibration of the vocal folds.

5.2.1 Extracting fundamental frequency

The fundamental frequency of a speech wave is reflected in several acoustic parameters. In a speech wave graph, for example, we can identify cycles of a wave and determine how much time it takes to complete one cycle. When we know the duration of a cycle of the speech wave (its period), we can calculate how many such cycles would fit into a second, and in this way we can determine the fundamental frequency of the wave at that point.

In a spectrum or a narrow-band spectrogram one can often identify separate harmonics (sine wave components into which a complex periodic wave can be analyzed; see section 3.2.4). The frequency of a harmonic is directly related to the fundamental frequency of the complex wave: the frequency of the fifth harmonic, for example, is five times the fundamental frequency. Also, the distance in hertz between two neighboring harmonics is equal to the fundamental frequency.

In a broad-band spectrogram one will often be able to see the individual energy pulses that are generated by the abrupt closing movements of the vocal folds. The time distance between two such pulses is equal to the cycle period of the speech wave.

A fundamental frequency graph records for successive moments of time the fundamental frequency of a speech wave. Time is normally plotted along the horizontal axis and F_0 along the vertical axis. An example is given in figure 5.1. The utterance displayed is: *Say boat again.* A speech waveform is shown in the upper panel and an F_0 graph in the lower panel.

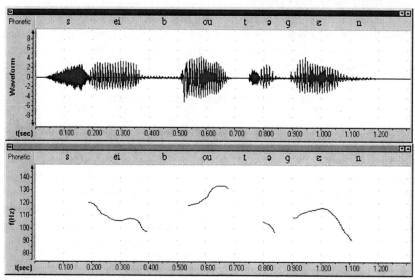

Figure 5.1. Waveform (upper panel) and F_0 graph of *Say boat again.*

The frequency range displayed along the vertical axis in the F_0 graph is 75–150 Hz. The maximum F_0 seen in this graph (during the word *boat*) is 135 Hz, and the minimum frequency is 91 Hz (at the end of the F_0 trace).

In the graph, there are interruptions of the F_0 trace, which occur during the consonants. This is expected for the voiceless fricative [s] and the voiceless plosive [t], because they are not associated with vocal fold vibration and their waves are accordingly not periodic. On the other hand, during the closure of the [b] and the [g], and during the nasal consonant [n], there is vocal fold vibration, as can be seen with some difficulty in the speech wave graph in the upper panel. The computer program with which this F_0 graph was produced, did not extract F_0 during these three consonants due to the weakness of the signal.

It is possible for a researcher to estimate F_0 at different points in an utterance on the basis of the acoustic parameters mentioned above. These estimates can then be recorded in a graph, and in this way an F_0 graph can be produced by hand.

The extraction of an F_0 trace from a speech signal by computer is a relatively difficult problem, and one that has not been solved entirely. A variety of algorithms for F_0 extraction have been developed, each with its own strengths and weaknesses. (An ALGORITHM is a complete and explicit, step-by-step description of a procedure. An algorithm can be expressed in one or another computer programming language. It can then be executed by a computer.)

F_0 extraction algorithms make use of one or more of the parameters mentioned above. Some algorithms look at the speech waveform and try to identify repetitive wave periods. Other algorithms apply spectral analysis to the speech signal and try to identify harmonics. Whatever method is used, none of them is guaranteed error-free, and the researcher therefore always needs to apply some common sense when looking at F_0 graphs.

One quite common mistake occurs when a cycle of a speech wave consists of two halves that are only slightly different from one another. An F_0 algorithm may fail to notice the difference between the two halves (understandably: due to the continuous movements of the articulators, two successive cycles in a speech wave are never exactly the same; F_0 algorithms therefore have a certain tolerance for minor differences when they are matching sections of a wave). If the algorithm fails to notice the difference between the two halves, it will think that each half is in fact a complete cycle, and as a consequence it will come up with an F_0 value that is twice as high as what it should have been.

Such an error is sometimes called an "octave error." An OCTAVE is a musical interval that corresponds to a doubling of the frequency. A possible way of limiting the number of such octave errors is to specify the upper and lower limits of the F_0 range for a certain speaker. A researcher may for example have learned from initial experience that the F_0 of a certain adult male speaker normally stays within 80 and 200 Hz. If this information is fed to the F_0 extractor, it will not be allowed to produce a value of, say, 300 Hz, even if it is tempted to do so. It will be forced to conclude that two rather similar wave segments are in fact the two halves of a larger wave cycle, so that it will come up with the correct value of 150 Hz.

At this point it is instructive to look at a raw F_0 graph as it is produced by the F_0 extraction algorithm employed by the SIL programs *CECIL* and *Speech Analyzer* (see figure 5.2).

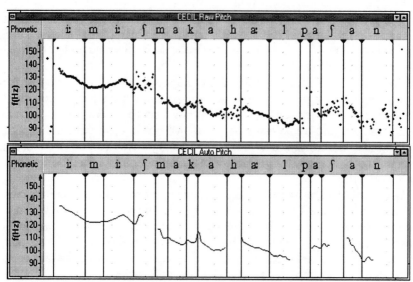

Figure 5.2.Raw F_0 analysis (upper panel) and final F_0 analysis of an utterance in Kalam Kohistani.

The raw F_0 graph is presented in the upper panel of figure 5.2, and a smoothed F_0 trace is presented in the lower panel. The vertical lines indicate segment boundaries, and a phonetic transcription of each segment is provided in the bar immediately above the graph.

The F_0 extraction program looks at one small section of the speech signal at a time. The size of that section is called the ANALYSIS WINDOW. The program tries to determine average F_0 for that small portion of speech, and then the window is moved a little bit to the right and the next measurement is taken. In this way the analysis window is moved in small steps from beginning to end through an utterance. (The step size is smaller than the window size, so that there is a partial overlap of successive windows.) The results of such a process have been plotted in the raw F_0 graph in the upper panel of figure 5.2.

One can see in the figure how for each time step of the analysis a dot has been plotted in the graph, indicating the F_0 measured at that point in time. During voiced and relatively loud stretches of the utterance, these dots occur close to one another, so that together they form a curved line. At other points in the utterance, there is no voice, or the signal is rather weak, and the F_0 extraction program had trouble identifying regular wave cycles. During such portions, the dots are more randomly scattered in the graph.

A second algorithm may be applied at this point, whose task is to find a path through the dots in the raw analysis, in such a way that a plausible F_0

trace is produced (this process is called TRACKING). The results of tracking are seen in the lower panel of figure 5.2. In places where the original dots are scattered too much, the tracking algorithm does not try to find a path through them. Where the dots are close together, it does. As a result we see a smooth F_0 trace that is interrupted at some points.

As should be clear by now, one should not blindly trust the F_0 extraction and tracking programs. Therefore, it is often good to check the F_0 trace of an utterance by ear. Especially when one has a facility for slow replay of an utterance (replay at, say, 50 percent of the original speed), it is not so difficult to compare the audible movements of pitch with what one sees in the graph. If there are things in the graph that do not seem to be correct, it may be useful to look at the raw F_0 analysis as well, and possibly also at the waveform of the utterance, in order to determine what is going on.

5.2.2 Interpreting F_0 graphs

Scales for displaying F_0

In a LINEAR SCALE display of F_0, one unit of distance (say 1 cm) anywhere along the vertical axis corresponds to a certain fixed F_0 difference in hertz (say 50 Hz). For instance, when a certain point on the vertical axis corresponds to an F_0 of 100 Hz, then a point 1 cm higher corresponds to a value of 150 Hz, and a point 1 cm higher yet to a value of 200 Hz. (These values are just examples, of course. They may be different in different F_0 graphs that you come across.) In figures 5.1 and 5.2, the scales used to display F_0 are linear.

It was said above that the human ear does not perceive F_0 differences in this way. A better approximation of human pitch perception is a LOGARITHMIC SCALE. On a logarithmic scale, a given distance does not correlate with a constant F_0 difference, but with a fixed proportion (ratio) of F_0 values. On a logarithmic F_0 scale, for instance, a distance of 1 cm might correspond to a doubling of F_0 (a proportion of 1:2). If a certain point on such a scale corresponds to an F_0 of 50 Hz, then a point 1 cm above it corresponds to 100 Hz, and a point 1 cm higher yet corresponds to an F_0 of 200 Hz. (Again, these values are just examples.)

It is quite common to display F_0 graphs using a logarithmic scale. When this is done, the SEMITONE is often used as the unit plotted along the vertical axis. Like an octave, a semitone is a musical interval. In fact, there are twelve semitones to one octave. A difference of one semitone corresponds to an F_0 change in hertz of roughly six percent.

Normally when we study F_0 graphs, we are not interested in absolute F_0 values, but rather in F_0 differences. On a semitone scale, the absolute values are normally meaningless (they are based on some arbitrary reference frequency, which is often taken to be 50 Hz). This is not a problem, as the absolute values are not linguistically relevant anyway.

One clear advantage of working with a semitone scale rather than a hertz scale is that it allows one to make meaningful comparisons between speakers that have different F_0 ranges. One may have a male speaker with F_0 normally between 80 and 150 Hz. One may also have a female speaker with F_0 ranging between 150 and 300 Hz. A difference of, say, 15 Hz in the speech of the male speaker will be perceived by the human ear as a greater difference than a difference of 15 Hz in the speech of the female speaker. On the other hand, a difference of, say, one semitone will be perceived as the same difference, whether in the speech of the man or the speech of the woman.

A semitone scale gives a good approximation of human pitch perception, but there are other scales around that are still more finely tuned to the way humans perceive pitch. An example of such a scale, which one may come across in the phonetic literature, is the Equivalent Rectangular Bandwidth (ERB) scale (Hermes and Van Gestel 1991). Another scale, the Bark scale, was already mentioned in section 3.3.1. As compared to the Bark scale, the ERB scale provides a better representation of human pitch perception in the lower frequencies (below 1000 Hz) and is preferred in intonation research, along with the semitone scale. The Bark scale is more widely used for scaling formant frequencies (involving frequencies that are much higher than the fundamental frequency.

F_0 ranges

One reason why absolute F_0 values are not linguistically relevant is, of course, that different speakers of a language have different voices with widely different ranges of F_0. The range of F_0 for each individual speaker mainly depends on the length and mass of the vocal folds. For males in conversational speech this range is typically between 80 and 200 Hz. For females it is typically between 180 and 400 Hz, and for young children this range can be considerably higher yet (Nooteboom 1997:642). In addition to the speaker's anatomy, language and culture, too, are factors that determine what range of F_0 values is used in speech.

In interpreting F_0 graphs, then, we are normally interested in F_0 differences, not in absolute F_0 values. When absolute F_0 values are given, these are only meaningful if we know what to compare them with. For instance, an F_0 of 185 Hz is relatively high if we know the speaker's F_0 range is 100–200 Hz. It is relatively low if we know that the typical range is 175–350 Hz.

Also, as was discussed above, when we compare F_0 differences across different speakers, it is more meaningful to express these differences in semitones or ERBs, than to express them in hertz.

Intrinsic F_0 of vowels

Within his or her range, F_0 movements are to a certain extent under the active control of the speaker. A linguistic researcher will be interested mostly in such actively controlled F_0 movements. The picture, however, may be distorted by fluctuations of F_0 that are not related to the prosodic features that we are interested in, but that are "the involuntary side-effects of other speech processes, often related to the production of particular speech sounds" (Nooteboom 1997:642).

A study of American English vowels by Peterson and Barney (1952) showed that high vowels such as [i] and [u] have a higher intrinsic F_0 than low vowels such as [ɑ]. Peterson and Barney's data were ten words produced twice by seventy-six speakers, giving a total of 1520 data items. Their findings were confirmed by Lehiste and Peterson (1961), who presented averages based on a set of seventy words produced by five speakers (a total of 350 data items), as well as averages based on 1,263 words produced by a single speaker. The results for Peterson and Barney's thirty-three male speakers, and for Lehiste and Peterson's speakers (who were all male) are presented in table 5.2. Note that the single-speaker F_0 values (last column in the table) are quite a bit higher than the other values, due to the use of another type of intonation contour.

Table 5.2. Average F_0 measured for American English vowels; from Peterson and Barney (1952) and Lehiste and Peterson (1961); F_0 given in Hz

Vowel	Peterson and Barney	Lehiste and Peterson (5 speakers)	Lehiste and Peterson (1 speaker)
i	136	129	183
ɪ	135	130	173
ɛ	130	127	166
æ	127	125	162
ʌ	130	127	164
ɑ	124	120	163
ɔ	129	116	165
ʊ	137	133	171
u	141	134	182
ə	133	130	170

There are some minor differences between the three columns of data in table 5.1, but the high (close) vowels [i, ɪ, u, ʊ] have the highest average F_0 in each column, while [æ, ʌ, ɑ, ɔ] always have the lowest average F_0 values.

In table 5.2, the difference between the highest and lowest average F_0 within a column ranges between 17 and 20 Hz. Expressed in semitones the maximum difference ranges between approximately 2 and 2.5 semitones. That kind of an F_0 difference is large enough to be audible to the human ear, and large enough to be employed by the tone system or intonation system of a language in marking distinctions of meaning (Nooteboom 1997:645). In other words, the size of such F_0 perturbations may approach the size of F_0 movements that are due to tone or intonation.

A researcher, then, should be aware that high vowels such as [i]and [u] may be intrinsically associated with a higher F_0 than low vowels such as[a], and that this factor may have a noticeable effect on the course of F_0 over an utterance. Such an effect may not be visible in individual utterances, but it may become apparent when one takes averages over a large number of items, spoken with similar intonation contours, as in the studies quoted above. While looking for possible tone or intonation contrasts, a researcher should be careful to "factor out" intrinsic F_0 of vowels, either by only comparing items that have the same vowel quality (or at least the same vowel height), or by averaging F_0 measurements over a large set of data.

Effect of consonant types on F_0

Lehiste and Peterson (1961) also looked at the influence of preceding and following consonants on the F_0 associated with vowels. They found that in general, higher F_0 occurs after a voiceless consonant and considerably lower F_0 occurs after a voiced consonant.

For one speaker, for instance, the average F_0 of the vowel [æ] (measured at the peak of the F_0 contour) was 170 Hz when it was preceded by [p], and 153 Hz when it was preceded by [b]. This is a difference of 17 Hz and approximately 1.8 semitones, which is a difference that is easily noticeable to the human ear.

The *shape* of the intonation contour, too, is influenced by the type of the preceding consonant: after a voiceless consonant, the highest F_0 peak occurs immediately after the consonant; after a voiced consonant, F_0 rises slowly and the peak occurs somewhere in the middle of the vowel.

Lehiste and Peterson did not find a regular influence of a following consonant on the F_0 of a vowel.

The effect of a consonant on the F_0 of a following vowel is often readily visible when one contrasts minimal pairs. An example from figure 4.5, is repeated here as figure 5.3.

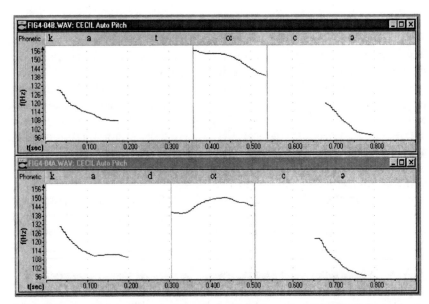

Figure 5.3. F_0 graphs of Dutch *Katootje* (a girl's name) and *kadootje* 'a present'; vertical lines demarcate the vowel following voiceless [t] or voiced [d].

The figure presents F_0 graphs of Dutch *Katootje* (a girl's name), with voiceless [t], and *kadootje* 'a present', with voiced [d]. In accordance with Lehiste and Peterson's description, the F_0 contour on the vowel following [t] (upper panel) is falling; the shape of the contour on the vowel following [d] is convex: it rises gradually to a peak relatively late in the vowel, and then starts to fall.

For the field linguist, the implications of the effect of consonants on F_0 are similar to those of the effect of vowel height. While studying possible tone contrasts or intonation contrasts, one needs to be aware of the influence of consonants on the F_0 of a following vowel. The best way to factor out such effects is to compare only items that have the same type of consonant in the relevant position.

Declination

A widely-observed phenomenon in the languages of the world is the tendency for F_0 to drift down gradually over the course of an utterance. This tendency is known as DECLINATION (the term DOWNDRIFT is more common among students of tone languages). Declination can often be seen when there are stretches of syllables in an utterance during which no linguistically significant F_0 changes take place. Pitch might be expected to stay low or high during such stretches, but in actual fact it slowly drifts down.

As a result of declination, a certain F_0 value (say 115 Hz) may be associated with a low tone if it occurs near the beginning of an utterance, whereas it may be associated with a mid tone or even a high tone if it occurs later in the utterance, when average F_0 has drifted down considerably.

Short utterances will often show one uninterrupted stretch of declination. However, in longer utterances the course of declination will at times be interrupted by a DECLINATION RESET (in tone studies people sometimes speak of UPSTEP). At a declination reset, the average F_0 is reset to the initial value and a fresh stretch of down-sloping average F_0 starts. Speakers prefer to let these resets coincide with important boundaries in the constituent structure of the utterance (Nooteboom 1997:648).

An example of declination is given in figure 5.4, which represents an utterance in Kalam Kohistani. A speech waveform is shown in the upper panel, and an F_0 graph in the lower panel. The F_0 range displayed is 80–160 Hz; a linear scale is used.

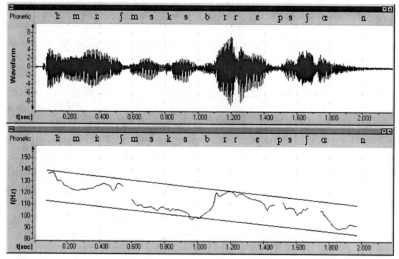

Figure 5.4. Speech wave (upper panel) and F_0 graphs of a Kalam Kohistani utterance; the two slanted lines show the trend of declination.

Two lines have been drawn in the figure; one line connects the highest peaks of the F_0 trace, and the other connects its deepest valleys. We may call these the top line and bottom line, respectively. Kalam Kohistani is a tone language with two contrastive levels: high and low. In this example, F_0 values near the top line rather neatly correspond to the high tone level, while F_0 values near the bottom line correspond to the low tone level.

The reader should compare figure 5.4 with figure 5.5. In the latter figure (which shows exactly the same waveform and F_0 trace as the previous figure) two straight horizontal lines are drawn at the maximum and minimum F_0 values that occur in this utterance. Again we can see the gradually declining trend of the F_0 trace over this utterance. At the same time it is clear that the sloping lines in figure 5.4 help a great deal with the identification of high tones and low tones, whereas the horizontal lines in figure 5.5 do not help at all.

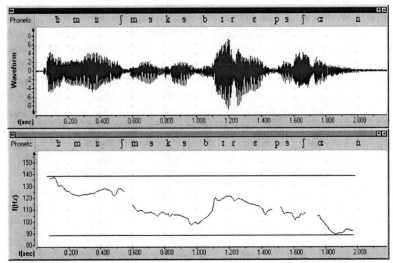

Figure 5.5. Waveform and F_0 graph, with straight lines marking highest and lowest F_0 in this utterance.

5.3 Duration and intensity

5.3.1 Duration

In acoustic phonetics, the term DURATION refers to the amount of time elapsed between the start and the end of a speech fragment (or a pause). Normally a researcher is interested in the duration of phonetic segments (vowels and consonants). Of course, the duration of smaller or larger fragments can also be of interest.

Durations cannot be measured if the starting and ending points of the units to be measured are not known. Therefore, a necessary preparatory step is the determination of the boundaries between these units in a spoken utterance. This step is sometimes called SEGMENTATION (dividing an utterance into segments). As speech is not a simple sequence of discrete segments, but rather involves a continuous movement of the articulators, with associated gradual changes of the acoustic signal, segmentation is often not a simple task. Some guidelines for segmenting a speech signal were discussed in section 2.4.2.

In the study of prosody we need to take into account that vowels and consonants have intrinsic duration. For instance, in section 4.2.1, we noted that voiceless plosives and fricatives are usually longer in duration than their voiced counterparts. Vowel durations, too, depend to some extent on the identity of the vowel.

Generally speaking, the vowel [ə] (schwa) is associated with a neutral configuration of the articulators. In an articulatory vowel diagram, schwa is normally seen in a position near the center of the diagram. Other vowels involve a movement of the articulators away from their neutral positions. Open vowels such as [a] and [æ] involve a relatively large deviation from the neutral configuration. It is not a surprise, therefore, that it takes more time to produce an [a] than it takes to produce an [ə]. Generally, open vowels tend to be longer in duration than close vowels, and vowels in the corners of articulatory vowel space (such as [i] and [u]) tend to be longer than related vowels closer to the center (such as the centralized vowels [ɪ] and [ʊ]).

While different vowels have their own intrinsic duration, vowel durations may also be influenced by the type of the following consonant. As Peterson and Lehiste (1960) observed, vowels are shorter when they are followed by a voiceless consonant and longer when they are followed by a voiced consonant. The shortest durations are measured before voiceless plosives and fricatives; longer vowel durations are measured before voiced plosives and nasals, and the longest durations are found before voiced fricatives. Using the same speech materials that were quoted above in table 5.1, Peterson and Lehiste (1960) determined average durations of vowels. Table 5.3 presents their results for six American English vowels. It is seen in the table how a higher degree of mouth opening corresponds with a longer average duration of a vowel.

Table 5.3. Average durations measured for selected American English vowels (from Peterson and Lehiste 1960)

Vowel:	ɪ	ʊ	ɛ	ʌ	ɔ	æ
Average duration in milliseconds:	180	200	200	230	310	330

Finally, phonemic length is, of course, an important factor influencing the duration of vowels and consonants. Many languages phonemically contrast long and short vowels, and/or long and short consonants.

A number of studies have been done regarding the perceptual threshold for duration differences. Some of these involved isolated sounds (speech sounds as well as non-speech sounds). In such studies, subjects listen to pairs of sounds and are asked to say which one of a pair is longer than the other. When these sounds are in between 40 and 250 ms in duration, perceptual thresholds are found ranging between 5 and 15 percent (one sound has to be 5–15 percent longer than the other sound for the difference to be perceived). Differences involving durations shorter than 40 ms or longer than 250 ms are less accurately perceived. Very short sounds (shorter than 20 ms) are not perceived as having duration at all. (In very short sounds, duration differences are perceived as loudness differences.)

Studies with speech sounds embedded in utterances are more difficult to conduct. It is reported, though, that the duration of embedded segments can be perceived with an accuracy that is at least as good as that found for isolated sounds. See Nooteboom (1997:654–656) for more extensive discussion of perceptual thresholds for duration.

Next to F_0, duration is an important acoustic parameter of prosody. However, durations in speech are not only due to prosody, but also to the properties of segments, as we have seen. Such segmental influences on duration need to be factored out when prosodic duration is studied.

5.3.2 Intensity

Intensity, sound pressure, and the decibel

As we saw in section 2.1.1, sound consists of small, rapid fluctuations of air pressure. These fluctuations have a certain size: they can be large or small. This size is called the AMPLITUDE of the vibrating air pressure, which is defined as the maximum deviation from average air pressure.

Naturally occurring sounds are usually complex: they do not involve a simple, smooth vibration of the air pressure, but rather they consist of many different vibrating movements occurring at the same time. All these different vibrations that together form a complex vibration may have different amplitudes. The complex sound signal itself may also be said to have an amplitude, namely the largest deviation that occurs during one cycle of the wave.

Two complex sound waves that have the same cycle amplitude may still differ as to the total amount of vibration energy that they contain. One can imagine a wave cycle that consists of one large fluctuation followed by a series of very small fluctuations. However, another wave's cycle may consist of a series of fluctuations that are all relatively large. Even though the size of the maximum fluctuation may be equal for both waves, the second wave contains more energy, and it would exert more pressure on, say, a human eardrum.

AVERAGE AMPLITUDE (or SOUND PRESSURE) is a measure that takes into account not only the size of the maximum vibration, but also of the other vibrations occurring in a complex sound wave. It is calculated over a section of a sound wave (an analysis window), which is usually 10 or 20 ms wide (normally enough to include at least two periods of a speech wave).

The conventional method for determining sound pressure is to take the set of deviations from zero occurring within the window, square each of these, take the average of the squares, and then take the root of the average. The resulting value is called the ROOT MEAN SQUARE (rms) of the air pressure deviations. When we move the window step by step from beginning to end through a spoken utterance, we can determine rms values at each step, and these can be plotted in a graph with time along the horizontal axis and sound pressure along the vertical axis. Such a graph presents a picture of how sound pressure changes over the course of a speech wave.

Another term that is used in this connection is INTENSITY (also called the power of a sound). Intensity is a measure of the amount of energy contained in a sound wave. Intensity is normally taken to be equal to the square of the sound pressure.

In sound pressure graphs and intensity graphs, values are normally given in DECIBELS (dB). A decibel scale is a logarithmic scale, which is a better approximation of how the human ear perceives intensity differences than a simple linear scale. We already came across an example of a logarithmic scale (the semitone scale) when we discussed F_0 graphs in section 5.2.2.

On a decibel scale, a difference of 10 dB corresponds to a 10-fold increase of intensity. This means that a sound of 60 dB has an intensity that is 10 times as great as the intensity of a sound of 50 dB. A sound of 70 dB has an intensity that is 10 x 10 = 100 times as great as that of a sound of 50 dB. At the same time, a difference of 20 dB corresponds to a 10-fold increase of the sound pressure.

Often, decibel values are calculated in comparison to a reference sound. Normally this reference sound is defined as the softest sound that a young, healthy human can still hear. It is arbitrarily assigned a value of 0 dB. Therefore, when it is said that a certain sound has a sound pressure level, or an intensity level, of 0 dB, this does not mean that this sound is in fact silence. Rather it means that the sound has a sound pressure level that is just at the threshold of audibility.

At the other end of the scale, the value of 120 dB corresponds to the level of the sound of a jet airplane for someone on the runway, or the level of amplified rock music for someone 6 feet away from the stage. Above that level we experience pain rather than sound. In the middle of the scale, at around 60 dB, we have the sound pressure level of normal conversation.

Note that one and the same decibel scale is used for representing both sound pressure and intensity. By convention, both the sound pressure and the intensity of the softest sound that people can hear are assigned the value of 0 dB. Likewise, both the sound pressure and the intensity of the loudest sound that people can hear without pain are assigned the value of 120 dB. Intensity and sound pressure are forced into the same scale, so to speak.

In figure 5.6, repeated from figure 2.5, the reader can see an intensity graph plotted over the associated speech wave. We see how, generally speaking, the intensity of vowels is greater than the intensity of consonants, and how within a vowel there may be fluctuations of intensity.

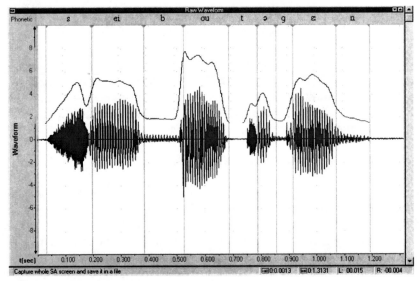

Figure 5.6. Signal intensity plotted over a speech wave graph.

Intrinsic vowel intensity

As was the case with F_0 and duration, a researcher of prosody needs to be aware that some intensity fluctuations are due to segmental effects, not to prosody. This was already clear from figure 5.6, where the intensity differences between most vowels and consonants are immediately apparent. However, there are also differences in intrinsic intensity among the vowels themselves. These may not be easily visible in one example, but when we take averages over a large number of speech items, some vowels appear to be associated with a higher average intensity than other vowels.

Once more we will quote data produced by Lehiste and Peterson (1960). Table 5.4 presents average intensities for selected vowels from American English. The averages are based on a set of 1,263 speech items (all monosyllables), recorded by one speaker on one and the same day, as much as possible on a constant pitch and with the same articulatory effort. The general trend is that vowels that are relatively open are louder (have a greater intrinsic intensity) than vowels that are relatively close.

Table 5.4. Average intensities measured for selected American English vowels (from Lehiste and Peterson 1960)

Vowel	i	u	ɛ	æ	ɔ	ɑ
Average intensity in decibels	75.1	78.2	79.3	79.4	80.6	80.2

Average intensity goes up from 75.1 dB for [i] to 80.6 dB for [ɔ], which is a difference of 5.5 dB. The smallest difference that we can hear is roughly 1 dB, and so we must conclude that the influence of vowel quality may have audible effects on vowel intensity, and that a researcher must take care to disentangle these effects from prosodic effects.

5.4 Analyzing prosody

In the previous sections we have looked at the acoustic parameters of prosody, namely fundamental frequency, duration, and intensity. In addition to these, distinctions of voice quality (such as regular voice, breathy voice, creaky voice) may also fulfill prosodic functions. Some acoustic aspects of voice quality (phonation type) were discussed in section 4.1.2.

The current section is concerned with the application of all this to the analysis of prosodic phenomena. It was already pointed out in chapter 1 that acoustic analysis does not replace normal procedures of linguistic analysis. Acoustic analysis can be useful, however, because (1) it can confirm what we have already heard with our ears; (2) it can provide another look at data that are causing trouble in the analysis; and (3) it can reveal significant distinctions that were missed in an ears-only analysis.

Acoustic analysis, then, functions as a supplement to linguistic analysis, not as a replacement of linguistic analysis. Therefore, before continuing, let me point the reader to a number of sources that provide further help with the linguistic analysis of prosodic phenomena.

A good introduction to the analysis of intonation systems is provided by Cruttenden (1997). Van Heuven and Sluijter (1996) present a useful review of the acoustic and perceptual correlates of accent (stress). An introduction to metrical phonology, which provides a tool for the phonological analysis of stress systems, can be found in several textbooks on generative phonology, such as Kenstowicz (1994). A good introduction to tone is provided by Yip (2002). A general overview of prosodic phenomena and their communicative functions is given by Nooteboom (1997).

5.4.1 Accent

Few areas in linguistics have witnessed as much terminological confusion as the area which is concerned with the relative prominence (strength) of syllables. In this section, I will follow a usage that is not uncommon among phoneticians.

I use the term ACCENT to refer to the prominence of a syllable in a spoken utterance, as perceived by a native speaker of the language under study. Accenting is something that a speaker does in order to make a certain syllable stand out among other syllables. As a result of accenting, a syllable can be said to be accented (or accent-bearing). Syllables that do not bear accent are said to be unaccented. There may be degrees of accent. In English, for instance, a syllable that carries the nucleus of an intonation-group is normally perceived as more prominent than other accented syllables within the same intonation-group.

Questions following from these definitions are: What do speakers do when they accent a syllable (what are the articulatory correlates of accent)? What are the effects of accenting on the acoustic signal (what are the acoustic correlates of accent)? How does a listener perceive a certain syllable as accented? What properties of the acoustic signal are the most effective cues to accent perception (what are the perceptual correlates of accent)?

The term STRESS can be defined, following Bolinger (1958), as an abstract property of a word, specifying a default "landing site" for accent. Major accents occur at certain places within an utterance for the purpose of focusing the attention of the listener on important information. Additional accents occur as a consequence of the rhythmical organization of the utterance. All these accents need landing sites. They need to be associated with specific syllables. When, for example, the word *America* is focused, an accent will be associated with the second syllable of that word, not with the third or any other syllable. The second syllable of *America* thus provides a landing site for accent, and for this reason it is said to be stressed.

In some languages stress can be contrastive. In English, for example, the only difference between the noun "(the) imports" and the verb form "(he) imports" is the location of stress. Such minimal pairs form a good starting point for investigations of the acoustic and perceptual correlates of accent. Accent will land on the first syllable if the word is a noun. It will land on the second syllable if the word is a verb form. How exactly is the accent distinction marked in the acoustic signal and how is it picked up by the listener? Can there be situations where there is no accent distinction at all (when the word does not carry any accent at all)?

As to the latter question, it is interesting to consider the reported phenomenon of "stress neutralization" in post-nuclear position (see e.g. Couper-Kuhlen 1986:24–25 and references cited there). In experiments, listeners appeared to be unable to distinguish (British English) *lóok-out* 'man on watch' from *look-óut* 'fault/risk' in: that's your *own* look-out (intonation nucleus on *own*). In such a case, there is an underlying distinction of lexical stress that is not realized in the form of accent on the one or the other syllable.

In the remainder of this subsection, we will review possible correlates of accent as observed in cases where there are perceptible distinctions of accent. The main source used for this overview is the article by van Heuven and Sluijter (1996).

Fundamental frequency

In studies of a wide range of languages, F_0 has been found to be an important phonetic correlate of accent. It is often believed that accent correlates with high F_0, but this is not necessarily true. Consider the following English dialog: "There is an elephant walking down the street!" "An èlephant?" In this example, the second speaker may express reluctance to accept the truth of what the first speaker said, by starting out on a medium pitch on the word *an*, dropping to a low pitch on the first syllable of *elephant*, and executing a rise from low to high on the last syllable of that word. Under this type of intonation contour, the accented syllable is associated with low pitch, not high pitch. Pitch on the accented syllable will even drop deeper as the speaker's incredulity is stronger.

A more accurate characterization is that accent is not correlated with just high F_0 or low F_0, but with a change in F_0. Even so, not just any F_0 change will be accent lending. For example, the final rise in the second utterance does not make the syllable *-phant* accented. As one researcher said (Van Katwijk 1974:5): "The strongest cue of accentuation will be found to be pitch, if it is shaped in specified intonation contours." Accent, then, correlates most strongly with specific types of F_0 change, called accent-lending pitch movements in the framework of 't Hart, Collier, and Cohen (1990).

The exact shapes of these accent-lending F_0 movements may vary from language to language. F_0 movements that are accent lending in one language may not be accent lending in another language, or may lend accent to another syllable. F_0 movements may be described in terms of their direction (rise versus fall), their size (which could be given in semitones, or in coarser categories such as full and half), and their timing. The latter may be specified relative to the onset of the vowel nucleus of the accented syllable, and can be given in milliseconds, or again in coarser categories such as early, medium, and late. In some cases one will want to specify the timing of the start of the F_0 movement (namely when pitch rises or falls within, or away from, the accented syllable). In other cases one will want to specify the timing of the end of the F_0 movement (when pitch rises or falls onto the accented syllable).

Accent-lending F_0 movements are assumed to be under the active control of the speaker. Van Heuven and Sluijter (1996) point out that there are also passive F_0 changes that correlate with accent. A syllable that is not associated with a focus-related accent-lending F_0 movement may still carry a lower degree of accent and stand out as prominent relative to its immediate neighbors. Such lower-degree accents may be associated with a small rising and falling F_0 contour.

The small rise in F_0 is due to increased airflow when the mouth opens for the vowel. The following small fall in F_0 is due to the narrowing of the vocal tract at the end of the vowel, which impedes the flow of air. The principle at work here (changes in the speed and volume of airflow through the glottis have an effect on F_0) applies to both accented and unaccented syllables. It is seen more clearly in accented syllables, however, since accent is associated with increased articulatory effort and, as a consequence, with increased airflow.

Duration

According to Van Heuven and Sluijter (1996), relative duration of syllables, more specifically of the RHYMES of syllables (the rhyme includes the vowel and any trailing consonants), is the most consistent correlate of accent in languages such as English and Dutch. Even when a word is not in focus and is not associated with an accent-lending F_0 movement, there may still be duration differences that mark a particular syllable as accented. An accented syllable is longer in duration than an unaccented syllable, provided that everything else is the same.

The lengthening effect of accent may be obscured by intrinsic duration, and by the effect of following consonants on vowel duration. Another obscuring factor may be pre-pausal lengthening (the widely observed lengthening of the last syllable before a speech pause). The best strategy, therefore, is to study minimal pairs (such as *ímport* and *impórt*) in fixed carrier sentences (such as "say the word _ again, please").

In such studies, absolute durations in milliseconds may not be very revealing. Instead it is better to look at proportions (ratios). For example, one can take the sum of the syllable durations within a word, and then express the duration of each syllable as a percentage of that sum. When words are produced by several speakers, or several times by one speaker, averages can then be taken over the percentages, rather than over the absolute durations.

One may then find, for example, that the first, accented syllable of a certain disyllabic word has an average relative duration of 70 percent, and the second, unaccented syllable an average relative duration of 30 percent. For the other member of the minimal pair (the one with accent on the second syllable) one may find that the relative durations are 55 percent for the first syllable and 45 percent for the second syllable. In both cases in this example, the first syllable is longer than the second, but what is observed is a shift in the proportions that correlates with the location of accent.

Intensity

It is often believed that accent (or stress) in non-tone languages is a matter of differences of loudness or energy, correlated in the acoustic signal with differences of intensity. This claim was tested in a number of perception experiments involving a range of different languages, the earliest of which were carried out in the 1950s (Fry 1955). In these experiments, the intensity of syllables was manipulated, as well as their duration and F_0, in order to see what effect there would be on the perception of accent. The stimulus material of the experiments consisted of minimal pairs of the type *cónvict* versus *convíct,* and the task of the listeners was to say whether they were hearing the one or the other member of the pair. The results showed that intensity is by far the weakest cue to accent perception, and that it is easily overruled by manipulations of syllable duration and F_0.

Acoustic studies do show that there is a correlation of accent and increased intensity (with intensity differences in the order of 5 dB), particularly in the case of accents that are associated with accent-lending F_0 movements. In the case of lower degrees of accent, these differences are smaller and less reliable. (The acoustic studies, like the perception experiments, involve minimal pairs, and compare a syllable in a context where it is accented with the same syllable in a context where it is unaccented.)

Van Heuven and Sluijter (1996:248) point out that a language is unlikely to employ such intensity differences for signaling linguistic meaning. Intensity distinctions as perceived by a listener are easily distorted by extraneous factors. When a speaker turns her head, or when some object (such as the speaker's hand) momentarily intervenes between the speaker's mouth and the listener's ear, the intensity of the signal may drop considerably. The magnitude of such intensity drops may be similar to the differences that are due to accent.

Spectral balance (spectral tilt)

When speakers expend more physical effort, as in shouting or in the production of an accented syllable, the effect is not only an increased average amplitude of the sound wave that is produced at the glottis, but also a change of the spectral composition of the sound. In spectral analysis, this change shows up as a boost of the higher harmonics. This boost is evident most clearly in the frequency range of 500–2000 Hz.

While we saw above that the overall amount of energy contained in a speech sound (its intensity) is not an important perceptual cue to accent, recent experiments have shown that the way this energy is distributed over the frequency spectrum is in fact a reliable cue to accent (see again Van Heuven and Sluijter 1996, and references cited there).

The spectrum of the sound that is produced at the glottis has a down-sloping trend (spectral tilt): the lower frequencies have higher intensities and the higher frequencies have lower intensities. The effect of shouting and accenting is that this negative slope of the spectrum becomes less steep. In other words, increased articulatory effort has an effect on the amount of spectral tilt.

It is not easy to measure such spectral effects. One would really need to look at the sound signal as it is produced at the glottis, so that the effect of the resonances in the vocal tract can be ignored. The technique of inverse filtering (see section 4.1.1) provides one way of doing this, but is too specialized and time-consuming, and therefore out of the reach of the field linguist. Van Heuven and Sluijter present a technique that is applied to the output speech signal. It can be used to make comparisons between items that involve the same vowel qualities.

This technique is carried out as follows: the speech signal is band-pass filtered, cutting off frequencies below 500 Hz and above 2000 Hz. (As was said above, 500–2000 Hz is the range where the energy boost that is due to increased physical effort is most clearly evident.) Of the filtered signal, an intensity graph is inspected and the peak intensity during the vowel under study is identified. This intensity is recorded in decibels. The resulting value is taken as a measure of the spectral tilt. On its own, this value is meaningless. When it is compared with measures taken from other instances of the same vowel, however, it turns out that a relatively high value correlates with increased physical effort, and a relatively low value with less physical effort.

Other phonetic correlates of accent

This discussion does not exhaust the possible phonetic correlates of accent. In a footnote, Van Heuven and Sluijter mention a study of English that showed that the duration of the intensity rise at the beginning of a syllable is another reliable acoustic correlate of accent. Intensity rises more quickly if a syllable is accented.

Yet another correlate is vowel reduction. Vowels in unaccented syllables may not be fully articulated, and as a result the quality of such vowels may shift in the direction of the central vowel [ə].

We have discussed accent and its effects on the acoustic signal at some length because of the complexity of the matter. It should be clear that accent (the perceived prominence of a syllable relative to neighboring syllables) is not related to one simple property of the acoustic signal. We have seen that certain F_0 phenomena are accent-lending: when they are present, the associated syllable is always perceived as accented. Even in the absence of accent-lending F_0 movements, however, syllables may stand out as more prominent than their neighbors. In such cases, longer duration and a smaller (that is a less negative or even positive) spectral tilt are probably the most reliable correlates of accent. Of these, duration is probably easier to measure.

In any case, because of the distorting influences of a multitude of other factors, absolute values for acoustic parameters are usually meaningless in themselves. Measurements for one speech item should be compared with measurements for other items in an intelligent way. The simplest way to accomplish this is to work with minimal pairs.

5.4.2 Tone

The languages of the world can be divided into tone languages and non-tone languages. The distinctive characteristic of tone languages is that words may have intrinsic melodic features. According to one author (McCawley 1964, cited in Fromkin 1978:3), tone is distinguished from other uses of pitch by its lexicalness. In this view, we speak of tone when a word (or a smaller meaningful unit such as a suffix or prefix) brings its own melodic characteristics to the utterance.

In a non-tone language like English, this is not the case. The shape of the F_0 contour with which a word is pronounced in English (for instance a rising F_0, followed by a falling F_0) is not tied to the word as such. It can always be replaced by another contour (for instance a stretch of low F_0, followed by a rise) without affecting the identity of the word, although changing the F_0 contour will normally involve a change of intonational meaning.

One way to test for the presence of tone in a language is to use a fixed carrier sentence (also called a FRAME) such as "could you show me the ___ once more?," and substitute many different words for the underlined blank ("could you show me the *table* once more; could you show me the *box* once more; could you show me the *apple* once more"; and so forth). In English the same F_0 contour (for instance involving a rising and falling F_0 on the substitution word) could be used for each of the resulting sentences. In a tone language one will find that, when put in the carrier sentence, some substitution words necessarily carry a different F_0 contour than other words in that slot (although this difference may not show up in each and every carrier sentence that is constructed). One may find, for instance, that many words carry a falling F_0, while some words are consistently spoken with a rising F_0. This constitutes evidence that the language is tonal.

If there is tone in a language, chances are that the different tones are contrastive and may be used as the sole distinction between different words or grammatical elements. Kalam Kohistani, a language of northern Pakistan, has many examples of this, such as *boor* 'lion' (with high tone) versus *boor* 'Pathan' (with low tone). Other languages may have tone but none or only very few of such minimal pairs.

The main acoustic parameter of tone is fundamental frequency. In addition, there may be distinctions of voice quality (register) accompanying distinctions of tone. Low tone, for example, may in some languages be accompanied by breathy voice, as both breathy voice and low F_0 are associated with a relaxation of the muscles in the larynx.

One may find correlations of tone and segmental structure. Such correlations are often due to the effects of consonant type (in particular the voicedness versus voicelessness of consonants) on a following vowel (see section 5.2.4). A typical example of such correlations would be a language were a vowel that is preceded by a a voiced plosive or fricative always bears a low tone, or starts out on a low tone.

It is said of some languages that they are pitch-accent languages rather than tone languages. The term pitch accent, like the terms accent and stress, is given a variety of definitions in the literature. In a prototypical tone language, tonal contrasts may occur on all syllables of a word. In a prototypical pitch-accent language, the language has only one lexical tone (or tonal melody), which may be associated with one or another syllable of a word, depending on the location of accent. Most tone languages are probably somewhere in between these two extremes.

It is possible that the acoustic and perceptual correlates of accent are different between non-tone languages and tone languages that have some kind of accent (including prototypical pitch-accent languages). Beckman (1986) found that duration and intensity are correlated with accent in a non-tone language such as English, but not in a pitch-accent language such as Japanese, where only F_0 is correlated with accent.

5.4.3 Intonation

Intonation involves the use of prosodic features for expressing communicative functions that are not tied to words, but relate to larger structures such as the phrase and the sentence. Within the framework of Cruttenden (1997), the analysis of intonation is broken down into three parts: intonational phrasing, nucleus placement, and the selection of the nuclear tone.

Intonational phrasing is concerned with the segmentation of speech into intonation-groups (called intonational phrases in some other frameworks). Intonation-group boundaries are established on the basis of phonetic evidence (pause, lengthening of the final syllable, declination reset), along with considerations concerning the possible internal structure of an intonation-group (one requirement for an intonation-group is that it must include at least one accent-lending F_0 movement).

Within an intonation-group, one accented syllable can normally be singled out as being the most prominent one; this is called the NUCLEUS. It is usually the last accented syllable in the intonation-group. The nucleus, as well as other accented syllables, are marked by a conspicuous F_0 change (F_0 rising or falling onto the accented syllable, or away from the accented syllable). The placement of the nucleus on one or another word within the intonation-group is important for determining focus (the marking of new or important information).

The F_0 contour that starts on the nuclear syllable and continues until the end of the intonation-group is called the nuclear tone in Cruttenden's framework. In English this can be a falling F_0 on the nucleus followed by low F_0 continuing until the end of the intonation-group. Alternatively it can be a falling F_0 on the nucleus, followed by low F_0, followed by a rising F_0 on the last syllable before the boundary. There are several other possible nuclear tones in English, as well. The task of the analyst here is to determine the inventory of contrastive nuclear tones of a language.

Intonation exists in non-tone languages as well as in tone languages. In tone languages, however, the number of intonational features employed may be less than in non-tone languages. Tone languages show intonational phrasing like other languages. At the edges of intonation-groups in tone languages, perturbations of lexical tones may occur. In Kalam Kohistani, for example, intonation adds a low tone at the end of declarative sentences. This low tone interacts with the lexical tone of the last word of the sentence. If the last tone is high, the combination with the intonational low tone will produce a falling F_0. If the last word carries a rising lexical tone, the outcome on the surface will be a low, level F_0, due to the influence of the intonational low tone.

Nucleus placement in tone languages may be a matter of a wider or narrower F_0 range (the F_0 distance between high tone and low tone), or of complete versus imcomplete realization of the lexical tones. A full realization of the tonal melody of a word, employing a wide range of F_0, is associated with the location of the nucleus. Absence of intonational accent may correlate with a simplification of the lexical melody, and/or with a reduction of the F_0 range.

The inventory of nuclear tones is highly reduced in tone languages, as the melodic shape of a word is lexically prescribed, leaving little room for intonation to add melodic features. As was observed just above, the edge of an intonation-group is the typical place for intonation to add melodic features, rather than the nuclear syllable.

References

Beckman Mary E. 1986. *Stress and non-stress accent.* Dordrecht: Foris Publications.

Bolinger, Dwight L. 1958. A theory of pitch accent in English. *Word* 14:109–149.

Couper-Kuhlen, Elizabeth. 1986. *An introduction to English prosody.* London: Edward Arnold.

Cruttenden, Alan. 1997. *Intonation.* Second edition. Cambridge: Cambridge University Press.

CSLU. 2008. *Spectrogram reading: Spectral cues for the broad categories of speech sounds.* Center for Spoken Language Understanding. Online. http://cslu.cse. ogi.edu/tutordemos/SpectrogramReading/ipa/ipadefault.html.

Fant, Gunnar. 1968. Analysis and synthesis of speech processes. In Malmberg, 173–277. Amsterdam: North Holland.

Fromkin, Victoria A. 1978. *Tone: A linguistic survey.* New York: Academic Press.

Fry, Dennis B. 1955. Duration and intensity as physical correlates of linguistic stress. *Journal of the Acoustical Society of America* 27:765–768.

Fry, Dennis B. 1968. Prosodic phenomena. In Malmberg, 365–410.

Fry, Dennis B. (ed.). 1976. *Acoustic phonetics: A course of basic readings.* Cambridge: Cambridge University Press.

Fujimura, Osamu, and Donna Erickson. 1997. Acoustic Phonetics. In Hardcastle and Laver, 65–115.

Goedemans, Rob, Harry van der Hulst, and Ellis Visch (eds.). 1996. *Stress patterns of the world: Part I: Background.* The Hague: Holland Academic Graphics.

Hardcastle, William J., and John Laver (eds.). 1997. *The handbook of phonetic sciences.* Blackwell Handbooks in Linguistics 5. Oxford: Blackwell.

't Hart, J. T., R. Collier, and A. Cohen. 1990. *A perceptual study of intonation.* Cambridge: Cambridge University Press.

Hermes, Dik J., and Joost C. van Gestel. 1991. The frequency scale of speech intonation. *Journal of the Acoustical Society of America* 90(1):97–102.

Heuven, Vincent J. van, and Agaath Sluijter. 1996. Notes on the phonetics of word prosody. In Goedemans, 233–269.

Kenstowicz, Michael. 1994. *Phonology in generative grammar.* Oxford: Blackwell.

Ladefoged, Peter. 1997. "Instrumental techniques for linguistic phonetic fieldwork." In Hardcastle and Laver 137–166.

Ladefoged, Peter. 2003. *Phonetic data analysis: An introduction to fieldwork and instrumental techniques.* Malden, Mass.: Blackwell Publishing

Ladefoged, Peter, and Ian Maddieson. 1996. *The sounds of the world's languages.* Oxford: Blackwell.

Lass, Norman J. (ed.). 1976. *Contemporary issues in experimental phonetics.* New York: Academic Press.

Lehiste, Ilse. 1976. Suprasegmental features of speech. In Lass 225–239.

Lehiste, Ilse, and Gordon E. Peterson. 1959. Vowel amplitude and phonemic stress in American English. *Journal of the Acoustical Society of America* 31(4):428–435.

Lehiste, Ilse, and Gordon E. Peterson. 1961. Some basic considerations in the analysis of intonation. *Journal of the Acoustical Society of America* 33(4):419–425.

Lisker, Leigh, and Arthur S. Abramson. 1964. A cross-language study of voicing in initial stops: Acoustical measurements. *Word* 20:384–422.

Lisker, Leigh, and Arthur S. Abramson. 1970. The voicing dimension: Some experiments in comparative phonetics. In Fry 348–352.

Malmberg, Bertil (ed.). 1968. *Manual of phonetics.* Amsterdam: North Holland.

McCawley, James D. 1964. What is a tone language? Paper presented to the meeting of the Linguistic Society of America, Indiana University, 1 August, 1964.

Ní Chasaide, Ailbhe, and Christer Gobl. 1997. Voice source variation. In Hardcastle and Laver 427–461.

Nooteboom, Sieb. 1997. The prosody of speech: Melody and rhythm. In Hardcastle and Laver 640–673.

Peterson, Gordon E., and Harold L. Barney. 1952. Control methods used in a study of vowels. *Journal of the Acoustical Society of America* 24(?):175–184.

Peterson, Gordon E., and Ilse Lehiste. 1960. Duration of syllable nuclei in English. *Journal of the Acoustical Society of America* 32(6):693–703.

Pike, Kenneth L., Ralph P. Barrett, and Burt Bascom. 1959. Instrumental collaboration on a Tepehuan (Uto-Aztecan) pitch problem. *Phonetica* 3(1):1–22.

Potter, Ralph K., George A. Kopp, and Harriet C. Green. 1947. *Visible speech.* New York: D. Van Nostrand.

Rietveld, A. C. M., and V. J. van Heuven. 1997. *Algemene fonetiek.* Bussum, Netherlands: Coutinho.

Shoup, June E., and Larry L. Pfeifer. 1976. Acoustic characteristics of speech sounds. In Lass 171–224.

Slis, I. H., and A. Cohen. 1969. On the complex regulating the voiced-voiceless distinction. *Language and Speech* 12:80–102, 137–155.

Stevens, Kenneth N. 1997. Articulatory-acoustic-auditory relationships. In Hardcastle and Laver 462–506.

Traunmüller, Hartmut. 1990. Analytical expressions for the tonotopic sensory scale. *Journal of the Acoustical Society of America* 88(1):97–100.

Yip, Moira. 2002. *Tone*. Cambridge: Cambridge University Press.

Van Katwijk, A. 1974. *Accentuation in Dutch: An experimental study*. Amsterdam: Van Gorcum.

Zanten, Ellen van, J. Damen, and Els van Houten. 1991. *The ASSP speech database*. SPIN/ASSP–report 41. Utrecht: Stichting Spraaktechnologie [Speech Technology Foundation].

Index

125

CPSIA information can be obtained at www.ICGtesting.com
Printed in the USA
LVOW121025110113

315304LV00001B/54/P